ALONG THE WAY

Taking Care of Each Other on Our Way to Heaven

God bless!

Stephen Douglas Williford

ISBN...

Stephen Douglas Williford © 2015.

stephenwilliford.com

Introduction

In October, Janet and I were in New Hampshire. The leaf color was spectacular. I loved walking in the woods with beauty all around. I guess I enjoyed it so much because I realized that the beauty would soon be gone.

My son and I were climbing up Sugar Loaf Mountain in the Arkansas Ozarks. The going wasn't too bad until the last hundred feet or so. Then it got scary. If you choose the wrong crevice to traverse, you place yourself in a dangerous situation. One false move and you fall off the side of the mountain.

For me, life has been like this. Maybe for you, too. Sometimes the going is easy and scenic. Sometimes it's fun. Sometimes it's exhausting. And sometimes it's ugly and scary. Or dangerous. Sometimes I have to take a different route. Sometimes I feel like the path is going straight up.

We had a good climb and a good time. Even if a little copperhead did wiggle between Hank's legs at one point. See, that's what I'm talking about. You never know what a day might bring.

But God tells us,

I am the Lord your God, who teaches you what is best for you, who directs you in the way you should go. Isaiah 48:17

God knows where we are and which way we should go. So, I decided to share a few stories and encouraging words with you. Wherever you are on your journey, I hope they will provide you with peace, encouragement and laughter.

See you on the trail,

Stephen Williford

A Cup of Cold Water Goes a Long Way

We were staying at the Buckhorn Inn in the Smokies. As we ate breakfast each morning, we became acquainted with another couple. Following breakfast, we found ourselves sitting next to them, in rocking chairs on the back porch, looking at Mount LeConte.

We learned this was their first time in East Tennessee. We enjoyed listening to their stories as they laughed at themselves for getting lost in the mountains or getting tired climbing up the mountains or both.

Our time to leave came far too soon. As we were checking out, I asked the front desk manager if I could buy the souvenir book about the Buckhorn and leave it at the desk for our new friends. Then we came home.

A few weeks passed, and I received a note from the couple, saying that when they heard a book had been bought for them, they both teared up. "The truth is," the note said, "we've had a very hard year. After a lengthy illness in which we had to be with her each day and night, my mother passed away. Business has been tough. And we've had some other issues. The trip to the Buckhorn was our first time to get away in a long while. Your kindness came at just the right time. We can't tell you how much it means to us. Every time we look at the book, we will not only think of you, but of the power others have to build us up when we really need it. Even strangers!"

The book didn't cost that much.
We didn't spend that much time with them.
But then, it doesn't always take a long time to show a kindness, does
it? Especially in our cold, impersonal culture, any kindness stands out.

• • •

A friend of mine has had a bad chain of events lately. He lost his job.
His wife asked for a divorce. He has been shunned by family members. His church family members don't know what to do with him or
for him.

It happened that I was going to have an estate sale. I asked him if he needed anything from what I was selling. I soon learned that he had nothing for the very modest apartment he found himself in. So, I gave him my old furniture, some pots and pans and Tupperware. Turned out that I didn't have to have an estate sale after all.

As I helped him move the furniture into his apartment, he thanked me and told me I was his hero. The furniture was vintage. That's a euphemism for old. I wasn't going to get that much out of the estate sale. I wasn't looking forward to it anyway.

• • •

There's a man who comes to my Wednesday night class at church. He's also in my Sunday morning class. I see him around the building during the week. As a matter of fact, his house backs right up to the church property.

"Do you know why I'm here?" he asked one day. I didn't.

"I'm here because Leon and Marilyn Sanderson, two members from your church, knocked on my door and wanted to tell me what the church was about to build." It happened to be a large Community Life Center, which he would be looking at through his back windows.

He and his wife welcomed them, and they quickly became good friends. His wife was suffering from cancer and died not too long afterwards. Throughout this time, Leon and Marilyn helped orchestrate whatever the couple needed.

The man had lived there for years and had never darkened the door of our church. Leon and Marilyn changed that with a knock on the door.

There's power in intentional kindness. More power than we can imagine.

It's taking the time to visit with the elderly person on your block.
It's choosing to say hello to that person at church whom no one is talking to.
It's writing a card to the person who has just lost a parent.
It's inviting the couple over that may not have many friends.
It's asking, "Is everything okay?"
It's putting $20 in that struggling person's hand and saying, "Go take your kids to eat some ice cream. My treat."
It's making a phone call to check on someone who is having a hard time.

We will never make a true impression in our communities until we are willing to regularly show kindness and thoughtfulness. In the midst of hatred and racism and injustice, God works through simple acts of thoughtfulness. Not too many people are going to retort, "Go away! Quit being nice to me!"
Jesus tells us that we will be rewarded for even giving a cup of cold water. You may not be able to do everything, but you do have water.

And if anyone gives even a cup of cold water to one of these little ones who is my disciple, truly I tell you, that person will certainly not lose their reward. Matthew 10:42

Enjoying Life Every Day

God wants us to enjoy life to the fullest. I'm not talking about skydiving or riding a bull named Fu Manchu. I'm talking about enjoying life each day.

Landon Saunders tells the story of being with E.H. Ijams once while they were going to visit a family in Arkansas. Dr. Ijams had been a college president and a minister.

As Landon and E.H. were walking up the steps in the snow to see this family, Ijams saw an earthworm wiggling across the snow in front of them. He stopped and said, "Landon, would you look at that? My, my, my little friend, you've certainly picked a cold day to come out!" He was 84 at the time. He enjoyed the simple pleasures of life.

A few years later, Ijams attended a dinner at my church. I was asked to take him home. It was my first time to meet him. He asked me questions the entire way. "Tell me about yourself," he said.
When he asked where I went to college, I told him David Lipscomb in Nashville. He did not find it necessary to tell me that he had served as president of that institution. Instead, as he got out of the car, with eyes gleaming and my hands in his, he said, "Steve, this has been an unexpected pleasure and delight. I have so enjoyed our newfound friendship. I hope this will not be our last time to visit."

E.H. Ijams stood out not just because he was good at what he did, but also because he found joy in each day.

Joy can mean different things, but in this case, I would like to suggest that part of joy is finding it in each day. We have to decide that we're going to find joy in each day.

Our walk with God allows us to have joy. Most people don't have it. Being joyful should not be dependant on our circumstances.

Finding joy in the ordinary. It's . . .

Telling one last bedtime story to your child or your grandchild.
Leading the kids on a lightning bug hunt.
Being the first one up, drinking a cup of coffee and watching the morning take shape.
Sharing the boat with family and friends.
Building a campfire and watching the flames.
Taking a walk around the block with your spouse or friends.
Taking time to admire the beautiful blooms in the Spring
Having a movie night with friends and family.
Sharing stories and news of the day around the table.
Visiting someone who needs visiting.
Reading that book you've been waiting to read.
Going to the plant sale.
Inviting someone over to eat.
Looking for someone new to meet at church.
Letting the dog sleep on the couch beside you.
Popping popcorn.
Lighting candles.
Surprising someone with flowers.

Living life to the fullest is a choice. It should be intentional. If you choose to find joy in the ordinary, you will. And by doing so, you'll not only be happier, but you'll enrich the lives of those around you.

But the fruit of the Spirit is love, joy, peace, forbearance, kindness, goodness, faithfulness, gentleness and self-control. Against such things there is no law. Galatians 5:22-23

Good Use of Your Day

I was leaving Sunday worship not too long ago. A woman stopped me and asked if I was me. I assured her I was. She gave me a huge hug and wasn't letting go. When she did, she had tears in her eyes.

"Over 30 years ago, you visited me in the hospital. You had seen an article in the paper about a terrible accident I'd had and you stopped in to say hello. You asked if you could say a prayer for me. I was so impressed with your concern and your faith. It made a difference in my life. I just wanted to say thank you."

I had not seen her since that day in the hospital. I had not thought of that meeting in a long time. I was in the hospital to visit a friend. Having read the article, I found her room and said hello.

• • •

A few years ago a nurse was taking care of my father in hospice. She saw me, hugged me, and wouldn't let go. "I'm Ann. You came to see me in the hospital."

I remembered it, but it had been at least 30 years ago, too. Ann had been in a horrendous accident, too. Her parents asked if I would visit her. She was in the hospital for several days, and I ended up visiting several times. I found out she liked music, so I brought my guitar. That's all I remembered.

"You let me get my anger out. You just sat in the corner and played the guitar. I could tell you cared about me. We even read the Bible some."

• • •

She came to my Wednesday night class and smiled during the entire class. After class she walked up and hugged me. Then she said, "You have no idea how much effect you had on my son. He had no father, but you went out of your way to help him in and out of class. I will always love you for that."

It's amazing how people remember when we reach out to them. You might forget, but they don't.

When Judy came to visit my father while he was in hospice, she asked if she could do anything for him. "Yes," he said. "I appreciate your card, but is that the only one I'm going to get?"

"How many do you want?" she asked.

"Oh, one a day is plenty," he said.

And that's what Judy did. She sent him a card every day for his final two months. She may have forgotten it, but I never will.

• • •

During that same time, Evertt Huffard, the dean of Harding School of Theology, came to visit. A lot of folks know him as Dr. Huffard. Daddy knew him as his backyard neighbor and fellow church member. About once a week, Evertt would come over and visit with Daddy. He would always give him a souvenir from a recent trip to the Holy Lands. Then Evertt would pray for Daddy. One day, I peeked in to see Evertt's head on Daddy's chest. Evertt was sobbing. He was truly hurting for Daddy.

Evertt may have forgotten those visits, but I never will.

Frank Maguire was a senior vice president for FedEx. I had been working with him on a project on Friday and he seemed somewhat down. So, on Sunday, as we were driving home from worship, I called him, just to say hello and see how he was doing.

I had forgotten all about that call. But years later, Frank reminded me of it. He said was going through a tough period and that call came at just the right time.

Dr. John Scott once pointed out to me that we remember who stands by us during difficult days. "They may not remember what you said, but they'll remember that you were there."

That's a wise investment of our time. I encourage you to join me in taking a few minutes to make that call, or write that card, or make that visit. There will never be a perfect time to do it. There will always be things that get in the way. We just have to do it anyway.

A few years ago, I helped Quint Studer write a book, *Hardwiring Excellence.* Quint had been president of Baptist Hospital in Pensacola, Florida, when it was in tough shape. All of their measurement scores were low. When Quint became president, one of the things he did was to write cards of thanks, recognition, and encouragement to the employees for thirty minutes each day. He *hardwired* that time in his schedule.

As he subsequently visited sick employees or employees that had passed away, he was surprised to see those notes were often framed and in a place of prominence. A note that took five minutes to write was kept for a lifetime.

I like that idea of building time into my daily schedule to reach out to others. After all, that's the only way it will get done. I want to make sure that I'm recognizing friends and family on a regular basis. I want to make sure that I'm keeping up with folks in my Bible School classes. I want to make sure that I'm keeping up with my neighbors and friends. And I want to make sure that I include them in my phone calls, notes and visits.

We have recently started inviting folks over for a meal. We try to average one family a month It doesn't always work that way, but I'm convinced the way you and I make a difference in this world is to reach out consistently. Not because it's thoughtful. But because that's what Jesus told us to do. To treat others like we would want to be treated. To treat others like we would treat Him.

Do not neglect to do good and to share what you have, for such sacrifices are pleasing to God. Hebrews 13:16

Live Life Harder

I went to a friend's celebration service today.

He lived in New York. I saw friends that I hadn't seen in a long time. Some since college. Some had come from New York. Some had come from the Gulf Coast. And the rest came from somewhere in between.

I was reminded of Bob's *love of life*. He was a professor of drama at New York University. He was an actor. He was a husband and a dad and a friend and a son and a brother. He enjoyed the company of those he loved and wanted to enjoy life with them.

They talked about Bob's *passion*. There was no in between. He either cared vehemently about a subject or he wasn't interested. But he was passionate about a lot of subjects. From politics to animals to movies to music to human rights. He could really get worked up about each subject. And, as his brother, David, said, he could really get irritated with you if you didn't understand why he was so passionate.

He was also not afraid to *step out and have fun*. I can remember being with him on a trip to Cherokee, North Carolina, to hold a Vacation Bible School for the young Native American children. One night, we were invited to come hear some local entertainment held in front of the grocery store. It was a group of cloggers. We had never seen this form of dancing before. The next thing we knew, Bob was up on stage, giving his best shot to clog with them.

David, told about a Halloween long ago when he and Bob went trick-or-treating around the neighborhood. Still in elementary school, David went as Zorro. Bob went as Superman. Just before they were to leave home to walk to school the next morning, Bob appeared in his Superman costume. When David told him he shouldn't wear it, Bob asked, "Why?"

As David explained, Bob did not care what others thought about the costume. He loved it and wanted to share it with his friends. David *did* make Bob walk about 20 feet behind him.

Finally, Bob *loved to laugh.* When we watched photo after photo of Bob on the screen, it was a laugh or a face for the camera. By watching these photos of Bob, it occurred to me that this was an element of his life that transcended the decades. His wife, Vance, said that even in his final days, he made people laugh, and laughed with them, in spite of his pain.

I have plenty to learn from that. *I need to live life harder.* I need to enjoy more sunrises, appreciate more birds, and let my kids know how proud I am of them more often. I need to be passionate about things that are important to me. I need to have more fun. And I need to laugh a lot more. If this is the day the Lord has made and we're to rejoice and be glad in it, I would think there should be quite a bit of laughter. I need it. You need it. It's medicine for the soul.

Vance told us that Bob loved to take nature walks in Central Park. Because of that, a bench was erected in his honor along a path. It will have his name on it. If you get to the park, I hope you'll look for it.

And I hope when you see it, you'll think about Bob. Look for a chipmunk or a squirrel. Think about what's important in your life and how you show it. And then do a little dance.

**I perceived that there is nothing better for them
than to be joyful and to do good as long as they live.
Ecclesiastes 3:12**

Special Plate

I was at a friend's house for supper. Her 7-year old daughter greeted me at the door, "Come on in, Steve! You're going to love this! *You* get the *Special Plate!*"

I smiled and told her that was great. I had no idea what the Special Plate was. When we sat down to eat, my young friend told me, "When you have the Special Plate, you get to go first!" So I thanked her and dished my food into a shiny red plate with white writing on it that said "You are special today."

After the prayer, she said, "And now we go around the table and say why we think you're special." This was not too hard since there were only three of us, and I assumed I would not be participating. The little girl went first. "I think Steve is special because he always takes time to play with me." Then her mother agreed and said, "I think Steve is special because he makes up stories for you."

When it was time for dessert - you guessed it - mine was served first. I was informed that since I had the Special Plate, I did not have to worry about clearing the table, returning food back to the fridge or placing plates in the dishwasher.

Although this was a new experience, I liked it. What's not to like?

They told me why I was special. It felt good. There are plenty of times when even those we care about take us for granted, or tell us what they *don't* like about us. The Special Plate gave an opportunity to be intentional about sharing compliments.

Since I was teaching school at the time, I made a Special Plate assignment for each of my students. Each had to create a Special Plate exercise for his or her family and write about it. Each had to bring a Special Plate to show the class. We took photos and put them up all over the classroom.

Over the years, I read close to 1,000 reports. Although not all were life-changing, some were. The students were astonished at the reaction of their parents when selected to receive the Special Plate. "I had no idea that something as simple as the Special Plate could cause my mother to cry," one student wrote. It was echoed by several others.

Many vowed to make the Special Plate a family tradition.

Okay, not every experience worked out perfectly. But a lot did.

As I continue to think about the Special Plate, it occurs to me, isn't that the way you and I are supposed to treat everyone?

The old lady in the gold car in front of you who is driving too slow.
The man at the store who wants to buy enough lottery tickets to keep you waiting in line too long.
The woman in Sunday School who talks too loud and too much.
The man in front of you who puts on his turn signal *after* he applies his brakes.
The woman in front of you at the grocery store who has the world's record number of coupons.
The parents who bring their crying baby to your daughter's graduation.
The person who works with you that always has to talk about herself at all times.
The kids in the neighborhood who ring your doorbell way too early in the morning.
The lonely widow who calls just to talk.
The relatives who are greedy.
The co-workers who think you're too young or too old.

I need to picture these folks holding the Special Plate. I need to concentrate on how to treat them in a way that makes them feel important.

Your homework, students, is to select or make a Special Plate. Have a Special Plate exercise at home at least once a month. Then, as you are out and about the rest of the week, picture the rest of us, holding a Special Plate.

Love one another with brotherly affection. Outdo one another in showing honor. Romans 12:10

Easter with a New View

Yesterday was Easter. We went to church with my mother at her retirement community. As I sat there with the 32 folks in attendance, one man sat by himself, his walker beside him. Hanging from his walker was his late wife's pearl necklace.

Another man used a magnifying glass to read his Bible. He died a few days later. I would be his pallbearer.

Since worship had not started, I decided to visit. I met a man named Roy. I asked how he was doing. He said, "I'm okay, I guess. My wife died six months ago. I have a big three bedroom apartment here. I'm lonely." Most, including my mother, were without their lifelong mates.

Maybe 10 in the group did not use their songbooks. They couldn't see, or couldn't hold the songbooks, or both.

There were no Easter baskets. No new dresses or ties. No Easter shoes.

There was no giddiness of small children who would soon be looking for Easter eggs. There was not the concern for getting to the restaurant early. There was not too much laughter.

These folks had simply lived a long time. They had outlived most of their friends. But, they were Christians.

Maybe you've heard the story about a preacher who asked the congregation to raise their hands if they wanted to go to Heaven. Everybody raised their hands except one man. When the preacher asked why he didn't raise his hand, he said, "Oh, I thought you were getting up a load today!"

I think if you'd asked, "Who would like to get on the bus for Heaven today?" most would have raised their hands.

They were thankful for Jesus' death and resurrection, and they were ready.

Later that afternoon, we went to the Baptist Trinity Hospice House to see a friend. His life over the last few years had been a mess - divorce, hurt feelings, struggles over who gets what, who lives where, and now he had cancer. He did not have much time for this earth. He was bitter and mad. The only thing he wanted to talk about was going home, being with his dogs, and feeling abandoned by what little family he had. They were not there on this holiday.

We invited him over to eat through the years and he never accepted. We had invited him to church over the years, as had others. He did come a couple of times, but that was it.

He reached the point where it was hard for him to talk, and when he did, I had trouble understanding him.

I wanted to talk to him about life and death. But he wasn't up to it. In one of his few moments of clarity, I asked if I could do anything.

He said, "Yeah, you can get in this bed and let me go home."

Heaven was not mentioned.

I was moved by his loneliness. A loneliness that age and circumstances can bring. But, as Jesus' followers, we're told by God that this stage is temporary. There are better times ahead. Conditions don't have to dictate our ability to celebrate God's love and promises for us.

The truth is, I think the residents at that retirement village had a better understanding about Easter than their adult children and grandchildren. They understood they would soon be taking the party upstairs. And they understood it was because Jesus came out of the tomb.

They understood they would soon be with their loved ones. They could kick their walkers out of the way as they kicked up their heels. They will be able to see clearly. They could take those hearing aids out of their ears. No tears. They were ready. They got it.

That's the view you and I need to have. Easter means life. Life forever.

He will wipe away every tear from their eyes, and death shall be no more, neither shall there be mourning, nor crying, nor pain anymore, for the former things have passed away. Revelation 21:4

A Time to Speak Up

It was my first semester to teach. I was the only teacher at school who taught only seniors. I had given my semester exams the day before and had just finished reading my daily memo from Melanie Semore, our vice president of academic affairs. In the memo, she encouraged the faculty to make sure we used the rest our exam week wisely. "Just because you've already given your exam doesn't mean your class should just have study hall for the rest of the week," she observed. "Begin a new chapter and finish the semester with a flourish."

With that in mind, I told my first period class, "Please turn to page 180 in your texts."

"You've got to be kidding!" a disgruntled student said from the front row.

I asked for clarification.

"Seniors don't actually have classes after we take our exam. We just do whatever we want."

Several of her friends vigorously agreed, and shook their heads at my ignorance.

I held up the memo and read directly from it. They informed me that this applied to everyone but the seniors. The students were quite willing to educate me on this time-honored tradition.

Then Kevin Lipe spoke up. "Mr. Williford. That's just not true."

Everyone glared at Kevin. It was not a popular statement to make. But it was correct. I remember the event like it was yesterday. And I will always hold a place in my heart for Kevin because he was not afraid to speak up and help me out.

The more I watch events in sports, hear comments on the morning talk shows, hear folks talk around the community, and listen to political opinions, I am more confident that I am going to have to stand up for what's true, even if I am the only one.

I just came from a men's prayer group. The speaker told us the latest survey said that about 20 percent of the people in our city go to church. He was telling us that because church buildings around the world are no longer being used; they have been turned into condominiums, museums, schools, and theaters.

We can see the change in the number of stores that are now open on Sunday. The number of people who mow their yards on Sunday morning. The number of young team sports that are played on Sundays. It's a new day for Christianity. We are in the minority. And we are not held in high esteem. Our spiritual beliefs are equated to a cult. We are considered ignorant, rigid, hate-filled, intolerant, stupid and unable to think for ourselves.

These days, if you disagree with someone's view about morality, you are labeled a monster, a villain, a hate-monger.

The Peanut Man

When you were young, perhaps you were afraid of bees or bugs or snakes or monsters or clowns. I was afraid of the Peanut Man.

When I was about three years old, my mother was shopping at Stepherson's Big Star in East Memphis. I was sitting in the shopping cart as we left. On the front porch entrance of the grocery, Mother said, "Oh I forgot something. I'll be right back," and left me. It was a different time, so leaving me wasn't the act of negligence it would be today.

As I sat there, waiting for Mother to return, something large lumbered out from around the corner. It was a giant peanut! He was walking straight toward me! He had arms and legs and was about 8 feet tall. At least that's what he seemed like to me.

My eyes got big, my mouth opened. I gripped the shopping cart. I had no idea what to do in the face of a giant peanut. He stuck out his white hand and I screamed. I evidently screamed so loud that Mother heard me, as did everyone else in the store.

She ran out the door and to the cart, explaining that Mr. Peanut was my friend. I would have none of it. I had enough friends. And none of them looked like a peanut. Mr. Peanut tried his best to shake my

hand, give me a hug and otherwise be friendly. I was petrified.

Later that month, when I went to visit my grandmother, she asked me to do something, and I dragged my feet. She then announced, "Do you know who is in the closet in this kitchen?" I didn't know anyone was in there.

"It's Mr. Peanut. And if you don't get a move-on, I'm going to let him out."

Jessica said it was only when the helicopter lifted off that she was able to breathe easier. One of the Seals gave her a folded American flag. "At that point," she said, "I began to cry."

As I read her recounting of the rescue mission in her book, *Impossible Odds*, and as I watched her interview on *60 Minutes*, I was struck with her pride, respect and gratitude for those Navy Seals. They did not know the outcome of the story when they jumped into the darkness that night to save her. They did not know they would all survive. But they were all willing to pay whatever cost necessary to save her.

That's close to what you and I are supposed to do every day. We don't have to look far to see people who are hurting. They are in our Sunday school class. They live next door. They stand by the traffic signal with a cardboard sign.

As I read Jesus' account of the man from Samaria who helped someone who was probably his enemy (Luke 10), I thought about how he didn't know the outcome of his story either. He didn't know if those robbers were still around on that treacherous, winding 17 mile road that dropped 3,000 feet from Jerusalem to Jericho. He did not know what would be required of him. But he responded to another's needs. And Jesus said that's how we should respond, too.

I find it interesting that we don't know the Samaritan's name. And we don't know the names of those Navy Seals. We just know they helped.

If you're in a rough patch right now, let others know. Someone will help. Not many, but someone.

When you go through a terrible time, you shouldn't have to go through it by yourself. Why? Because God said so. Because you are a child of the King. Because the *Supreme* Commander in Chief gave the order to help you.

And when you're over your troubles, join me in watching out for others. We need to take care of each other on our way to Heaven.

I'm sure that Samaritan had plenty of other things to do. He had his own set of problems. He had not always been treated right. His life had not played out perfectly. He had his share of critics. But maybe he knew that conditions are never perfect to do good.

Conditions weren't perfect for Jesus. He didn't say, *Today is a good day to stay in Heaven.* He didn't say, *This is not a good day to be beaten, betrayed and killed.* He didn't say, *This is not a good day to die and be the sacrifice for the entire human race.*

He just did it.

Did it ever occur to you that Jesus may have been thinking of himself as the Good Samaritan, and you and me as that man in the road?

Jesus lets you and me know that we need to learn from the story of the Samaritan.

Our role is to love others as we come across them.

And do whatever it takes to help them.

That's all we can do. Just be a good neighbor. You and me.
We don't know everything that's happened to Jessica Buchanan since her rescue. We don't know where those Navy Seals are now.

Got cancer? Get in the truck.
Lost your job? Get in the truck.
Have family problems? Get in the truck.

I'm not leaving you. You're not leaving me. We're in this thing to-gether until our final breaths.

Get in the truck.

Share each other's burdens, and in this way obey the law of Christ. Galatians 6:2

Hold On!

As Hank and I made our travels to camp or fish, we often saw turtles trying to cross the road. Hank insisted that we stop the car to help the turtle safely get to the other side. He also nursed some injured turtles back to health. He saved a lot of turtles that way.

Maybe you can identify with those turtles. You find yourself in a tough spot. There is trouble in every direction. No end and no help in sight. The going is slow. You feel helpless. You recognize that you can't get out of your predicament by yourself.

It's a terrible, lonely place to be.

I can only remind you that *God is aware of what's going on.* One of my favorite verses is from Psalm 34:18.

God is close to the brokenhearted
And those who are crushed in spirit.

Remember that verse. God cares about you and will help you. Don't give up.

Find some good Christian men to hang out with. Men of integrity. Men who are good examples. Men who are upbeat and encouraging. Men who are compassionate. Men who trust God. Go to church with them. Go to Sunday School with them. Watch movies with them. Or games. Or eat lunch. Just be around them.

Get outside. Feeling the sunlight is good for you. Walk or ride your bike, and do it regularly.

Get a Bible that you can mark up. Turn to Psalms. Read three psalms a day. Highlight everything you can identify with or that speaks to you.

Pray. Tell God exactly how you feel. He knows what you think anyway. If you're mad at Him, say so. If you don't understand, say so. If you feel like He is not helping, tell Him. Do this at a regular time. This is a style of prayer, by the way, that you see all through the Bible. Some call it a lament. God will not strike you down for being honest with Him!

Recognize your need for God. Jesus said that those who are poor in spirit are blessed. He didn't mean happy are those who have little spirit. He meant that the beginning of faith is to realize that you can't make it without God's help.

Finally, **Hold On!**

When I was a senior in high school, I was looking forward to a great summer job. It was being a camp counselor at Camp Rock Creek in Norman, Oklahoma. I couldn't wait.

In the first week of May, the camp director, James Robinson, called and asked if I happened to be a lifeguard.

I responded that I was not. He asked if I could swim, and asked me about my swimming history. I thought these were odd questions but I told him that I had achieved the Mile Swim Award in the Boy Scouts and had a Swimming Merit Badge. He paused and said:

"Okay, here's the deal. It turns out that one of our camp lifeguards can't come to camp this year. Since you are the new counselor, in order for you to still come, we need for you to not only be a counselor but also a lifeguard."

I thought about that for a minute. Since I was not a lifeguard, I seemed to be out of a job before I even started.

"So, I have checked, and there is an intense American Red Cross Lifeguard training class that starts this Monday. It meets every day for three weeks. It will give you the certification that you need to come to camp and be a lifeguard."

Out of the jaws of defeat, it seemed I now had my job back.

"But you have to have that certification."

So on Monday, I showed up at the Mason YMCA in Memphis to begin the class. When I sat down on the pool's edge with the 10 other class members, I noticed that everyone else was wearing red swimming trunks. Additionally, everyone else had a crew cut.

When the instructor appeared, he looked like a professional wrestler. He was about 6'3" with muscles in every direction. He, too, was wearing red swimming trunks. He, too, was wearing a buzz cut.

"My name is Sergeant Wallace," he boomed.

I had never met anyone named Sergeant. It seemed like a strange first name. Maybe it was a family name. He was probably the only Sergeant in his class.

"For the next three weeks, you will train on how to save lives. At the end of those three weeks, you will have a final exam. For the final exam, I will swim out to the deep end of the pool. At that time, you will either rescue me or I will rescue you. Any questions? Good. Let's begin."

The rest my classmates said something in unison that sounded like "Hoo Rah!" It was at this moment that I realized that I was in the middle of a United States Marine Lifesaving class. I later learned I had received special permission, given my situation, to participate.

So, for the next three weeks, we learned how to perform lifeguard techniques. We worked hard. Then it was time for the final.

I had not been able to eat all day. These guys were all Marines. I had just graduated from high school three days ago. This was an important and overwhelming test. In order for me to go to Camp Rock Creek in less than a week, I had to pass it.

The class members, with their red swimming trunks, sat on the edge of the pool. Sergeant Wallace leapt into the water, stroked out to the middle of the deep end and said, "When I call your name, you *will* enter the water and proceed to my location. I will allow you to secure a hold on me. Your mission is to get me to the side of the pool. If you are able to touch the side of the pool, you pass. If you are not able to

To Make a Difference,
You Must Spread Cheer

It all started when John Martin's dog, Tiger, became sick. The vet told him to take Tiger on short walks, stopping often. To John's amazement, when they stopped, people waved. So he waved back.

Tiger eventually needed to rest more than walk. So John stood with Tiger at the corner of Walnut Grove and Holmes in Memphis every morning from 7:30 to 9:00 and waved to folks going to work and children going to school. He did this for years. He was not crazy. He was a retired train engineer. As a matter of fact, his wave, right hand extended sideways and shaking rapidly, was an engineer's wave.

He became a legend. People wanted to see this man on the corner. When asked by reporters why he stood there and waved, he explained that everybody had problems. He tried to think of how he could help, and it was overwhelming. It was also depressing to think of doing nothing. *So, he decided to spread cheer.* He knew that many people dreaded going to work. He knew that everyone hated traffic. He understood that moms were fighting with their kids as they were nearing school, and that kids were dreading another day of drudgery. So he did what he could.

He said he didn't have money. He was too old to help anyone in a physical way. *So, he decided to spread cheer.* He waved. Tiger wagged his tail. As days turned into months, folks returned his wave. They returned his smile. They said hello to his dog. Some commuters reported they went out of their way just to say hello to the man who spread cheer. He was asked to come on the *Late Show with David Letterman* to explain his rituals, thus spreading the joy to a nation.

He was out there every day in his shirt and tie, with a hat, despite the season and despite how he felt. People said they felt better just from seeing this single individual wave and smile at them. Why? *Because he was often the only person that waved and smiled at them all day.* He was honestly glad to see them. Going and coming. He also came back out from 4:00 to 5:30.

When Tiger passed away, Mr. Martin stood on the corner by himself,

waving.

His mailbox was flooded with sympathy cards. Someone placed a wreath at the corner. Dozens of well-wishers offered puppies. He finally accepted a puppy from the Memphis Humane Society, a collie mix he named Choo-Choo.

When he had pneumonia, Mr. Martin's mailbox filled up again. When he reappeared on the corner, motorists stopped to offer him cards, coffee, dog food, even a new leash.

Mr. Martin finally had to stop waving about a year before he died. I'd like to think that his house was flooded with cards and flowers and doggie treats.

I do know that he spread cheer in its most basic form. As you read this, you might be thinking, "He *was* crazy. Who else would do something like that?" I'll grant you that it was unusual behavior. Does the fact that he wanted to spread a little cheer to people make him crazy?

Let me flip the table on you. What do *you* do that spreads cheer?

Are you intentional about being a joy giver? Do you spread cheer on a daily basis? If this is the day the Lord has made, how are we supposed to rejoice and be glad in it? In the privacy of our homes? I don't think so.

If I have the *joy-joy-joy-joy down in my heart,* shouldn't I be passing it around to those who don't have that kind of joy? Maybe not the way John did it, but somehow, someway in a consistent, persistent manner?

To make a difference, you and I have to spread cheer.

We have to learn how to intentionally smile. To find every opportunity to laugh. Life has enough ripples. To truly enjoy this good life that God has given us, we must have joy and share that joy as much and as possible.

So, if you happen to see an old codger waving at you from the corner, slow down and wave. This idea is growing on me. Could I borrow your dog?

Let all that you do be done in love.
I Corinthians 16:14

The Art of Missability

Today makes six years since he died. By the time, you read this, it will be longer.

He was and is my father, Henry Williford. No middle name.

He was my greatest supporter. My greatest cheerleader. Always ready to listen and always eager to help in any way possible.

He was always positive and kind and present. He always had a smile, something funny to say, a compliment, a hug. He always was thrilled with my presence.

He treated my mother like a queen. He was in constant contact with her. He would rather be no place else than in her presence. He was quick with compliments for her.

The profound advice that he gave me occurred after his death. Want to be remembered and missed? **Do something missable.**

Love others with the kind of passion that makes them tangibly know when that love is gone.

Be so involved in the lives of those you love that they appreciate you more and more, even after you have left this world.

Don't get bogged down in jealousy, little disputes, placing worth on what you have, petty criticisms, sarcasm, all-about-me-ism, and negativism. Replace that with pure, radical, consistent, transparent love.

It's a love that leaves a hole in the heart. But it's a good kind of hole. It means you hit the bullseye.

The purpose of love is not to cause people to miss you. But it's one form of measurement. It's how you know that you touched someone's heart.

I think Daddy would like the fact that I'm using his passing as an example. An admonition to love with all you have while you are here.

My son, Hank, and I went to the Ocoee River a month ago to shoot the rapids on a raft. Daniel, our guide, asked, "Do you want to really go for it or hang back a little?"

Before I could answer, Hank said, "Go for it." I was content with hanging back and enjoying the scenery.

I learned that meant going right through the boiling water instead of going around it. When other boats were steering around to the side, we were in the middle of the spray so high that no one could tell if we capsized or not.

Being on this side of the trip and seeing that we didn't die, I think it was great. Hank said it was the most fun he'd ever had.

We went for it.

I love to see the mountains covered with snow. When it's not too crowded, I love to ski at places like Steamboat Springs or Snowbird. I have found that since I don't get to ski much, I tend to have trouble navigating in a crowd down steep hills.

The views are spectacular. I enjoy hearing the sound of skis on the snow and feeling the skis make new tracks over new snow. The feel of the cold air on my face, the view of the mountains, the smiles on my family's faces . . . we've had some wonderful memories.

And then there's the skier who is not out for enjoyment. He is out to set a record. He's out to prove a point. He's out to be seen. He's out to show no fear.

This is the skier who does not zig and zag down the mountain. He goes straight down, regardless of the degree of difficulty. Sometimes he barely misses another skier making the horizontal cuts. As he continues down the steep mountainside, he picks up speed. His knees are bent, his poles are tucked and he is looking straight down the slope.

And then it happens. He hits a bump. Maybe not a huge bump. But at his speed, it is just enough to disrupt the trajectory. Although he tries to correct the problem, it doesn't work. The next thing you see is a skier who has gone airborne. Then he becomes a snowball. Skis go in two directions. Poles go in two other directions. Goggles fly in the air. A knit cap shoots up in the air. A scarf drifts into the turbulence. And maybe even a boot or two.

When the snow clears, stuff is strewn everywhere. Including a body. It is quite a sight. It looks like a deadly yard sale.

Although I don't recommend this course of action on the slopes, I think Jesus is asking you and me to live life like a yard sale. We are to live life, holding nothing back. We are to give Him everything we have. Anything we do for God must be our very best. Jesus tells us:

You shall love the Lord your God with all your heart, and all your soul, and all your mind. Matthew 22:37

That's the radical kind of love Paul talks about in I Corinthians 13.

Going for it.

Loving with all you've got. So that when you're gone, people notice the lack of that love in their lives.

That's loving with all your heart, soul, strength and mind.

That's what God wants you to do.

Not half way. Not just on birthdays and holidays. Not just on a mission trip or church function. Not when you're in the mood.

Day in and day out.

Who to target?

Start with the folks closest to you. Make sure you've got that right. It's a daily thing. Set the pace for loving words and actions. Set a world's record in being kind. Write the card. Attend their ballgames, recitals and concerts.

Then move to those you go to church with, your neighbors, your co-workers.

It won't be convenient. It won't always be pretty. It may be boring. It sometimes won't even be acknowledged or appreciated.

But it's what God says you and I need to be about to make a difference.

My life is not perfect. Far from it. But I want to make such a difference in the lives of others, that when I'm gone, I'll be missed.

That means being my children's greatest supporter, whether they want to spend time with me or not. Whether they recognize it now or not.

That means being kind to those who have not been kind to me.

That means showing up to share happy times and sad times in the lives of my friends.

That means being thoughtful enough to make the phone call and write the note, whether I ever get a card or call in return.

That's not always easy. I want to say, "Why don't you say thank you a little more often? What about me?" I don't like being taken for granted.

And then I think of all the times my father could have said that about me.

But he didn't. It's a judgment call, but I think the important thing to him was to let me know that he loved me unfailingly, that he was

proud of me day in and day out, that he was physically there to support me in any endeavor, and that there was nothing he'd rather do
than spend time with me.

He loved me more than anyone ever has. That's why I miss him more than anyone else.

But here's the interesting thing. Other people feel that hole, too. My children, my mother, his friends and relatives. There was a hole that was left because there was no longer that presence of love and support. But there was a memory of it.

That seems like a good blueprint for me.

A Sunday school class from our church erected a bench in his honor in the middle of a little garden on the church grounds. Whenever I want to talk to Daddy, I don't go to the cemetery. He's not there, anyway. I go to his bench. I talk to him like he was sitting on the bench with me. I give him updates on my life and fill him in on Brittney and Hank. I tell him about decisions I have to make, disappointments with family members and even some funny things that occurred. I tell him about Mother.

I tell him that I love him and I miss him. And I thank him for loving me so much and that I miss him so much.

A new command I give you: Love one another. As I have loved you, so you must love one another. By this everyone will know that you are my disciples, if you love one another. John 13:34-35

Simple Is Good

It is April 28. Hank and I had a good weekend. We took the Bass Tracker out for the first time this year. We caught some catfish, small-mouth bass, and some largemouth bass. Hank caught a largmouth that was about five pounds.

In the middle of the day, shade was at a premium. We found an old abandoned dock located where the Pickwick State Park Inn used to be. We connected to it, got the chairs out and ate lunch. With lines in the water, we discussed life. It was a good place for a father and son to share time together.

The next day, we went to the little church close to where our farmhouse is. There was no praise team, no praise band, no PowerPoint and no videos. Just worship with about 130 others. The singing was spirited. The communion was sincere. The sermon was challenging. Several welcomed us.

On our way back to the house, we commented on how good the service had been. And it shared something in common with the day before. It was simple and from the heart.

I like simple. I guess that's why I like fishing. And hiking. And sitting on the porch. I don't have to go to Disney World to enjoy life.

And I don't have to have a lot of electronics to worship.

It got me thinking. What does God want? How does He want you and me to live?

And what does the Lord require of you? To act justly and to love mercy and to walk humbly with your God. Micah 6:8

Not very complicated. There are many take-aways from a passage like that. Here's mine for today.

To act justly. To live in the light. To love God and to love others. Our job is to act honorably, truthfully, and fairly, and to consider the interests of others above our own.

To love mercy. God has given us grace to be able to cross a bridge into Heaven. We have sinned and fallen short. He has given us a pass to live with Him forever. For that reason alone, we have to be merciful to others. To our relatives, to our friends, to our employees, to our bosses, to our neighbors and to those who don't like us.

To walk humbly with our God. Jesus called it Poor in Spirit. We must constantly be aware of the fact that we cannot make it on earth or to Heaven without God. With God all things are possible. Without Him, nothing is possible.

Life can get complicated. It seems to me that we need to keep it as simple as possible. I have heard the statement, The main thing is to keep the main thing the main thing.

church building since we've met.

Harvey loved my father. He was a hard worker, not given to take breaks, despite the temperature, weather, season or time. But he made an exception with my father. He would sit on the porch and talk to Daddy for an hour. He would bring Mother and Daddy tomatoes by the dozen. He treated Daddy like his own father, I think.

Harvey liked to have the house and grounds looking good when he knew Mother and Daddy were coming. Often, there would be a bowl of fruit or vegetables on the table for them.

Harvey saw the signs that Daddy was sick. He spent more and more time with him during those final visits. A few weeks after Daddy died, Hank and I went up to Saltillo and spent a few days. Harvey came one morning to do some grass cutting and weed eating. I went out to visit with him. His skin was weathered and dark from the sun.

After we talked for a bit, Harvey looked up at me and said, "I want to tell you something. I sure am sorry about Mr. Henry. I miss him. If I could have traded places with him, I would have."

I think that was one of the most touching things anyone has ever said to me about Daddy's death. Harvey was completely serious. That's why it meant so much. He loved my father so much that he was willing to trade his healthy life for Daddy's life of terminal illness. I don't recall anyone else making the same offer.

We're told that the greatest love is when one person will lay his life down for another. I have no doubt that Harvey meant what he said. He always does. It got me to thinking. I would do the same for some family members. Maybe a friend or two. That's where it stops. Not other church members. Not neighbors. And, no offense, not you.

I don't think that's the way it's supposed to be. I'm supposed to have a greater love. A higher love.

I wish Harvey could speak at church. I have much to learn.

Greater love has no one than this, that he lay down his life for his friends. John 15:13

Celebrate Today

I had the occasion to visit with some health care professionals who work in hospice. Hospice takes care of patients with an expectation of only a few months of life. It's a wonderful program, full of unselfish caregivers, and I highly recommend it to you and your family.

We were talking about the new Hospice House, built for patients who were not able to stay in their homes. We were particularly talking about the perception of the Hospice House. It is no secret that hospice is associated with death. As a matter of fact, some families won't accept hospice because they feel it is the recognition that death is close. And, there was a concern that the Hospice House could be perceived as a place where folks go to die.

The question: how can we change this perception? My thought was that hospice professionals should simply speak honestly and compassionately. And intentionally. So, I suggested saying:

Mr. Smith, if things go the way the doctors say, your time on earth may be limited. On the other hand, I could get hit by a bus on the way home tonight, or hit by lightning, or choke on an M&M or get bit by a poisonous spider. I don't have a lot of control over that. But what you and I do have control over is today.

We can choose to think about death and other things we can't control, or we can celebrate today. And, when you think about it, that's all we have ever been able to do. I want to make today the best day of your life. And tomorrow, better than that. I don't know how much time either one of us has, but let's celebrate the time that we do have.

Ever since those conversations, I have tried to adopt that philosophy for each day of my life, regardless of what I face.

This is the day the Lord has made. Let us rejoice and be glad in it. Psalm 118:24

How Forgiveness Works

Ronn and Susan Rubio were leaving for the evening. The last thing Ronn said to his sons before they left was, "Boys, don't play baseball in the backyard. You know what happens every time you get a game going. A window gets broken."

The boys promised they wouldn't. But after a little while, they couldn't stand it and went outside to play. And it wasn't long until David hit a line drive right through the den window.

When Ronn and Susan came home, David immediately confessed his transgression. Ronn and Susan both expressed their disappointment that he had disobeyed them. Ronn told him that the money to fix the window would come out of David's allowance until it was paid for. Then Ronn said:

"Okay, you made a mistake. You said you were sorry. We've agreed on a punishment. So, now it's behind us, forgiven. Have a good night, son."

David tossed and turned all night. The first thing the next morning, he rushed in to apologize to Ronn and tell him again how sorry he was for disobeying him.

"What are you talking about?" Ronn asked.

"What do you mean, what am I talking about?" David asked. "I'm talking about the window I broke."

"When we spoke last night, did I say it was forgiven?" Ronn asked.

"Yes."

"Oh, okay. That's why I don't remember. When something is forgiven, it's also forgotten."

"That's crazy! It just happened yesterday. How can you *not* remember that?"

"I am forgiving you the way God forgives us, and the way I want you to forgive others."

Is God's forgiveness that simple? Consider these scriptures:

No more shall every man teach his neighbor, and every man his brother, saying, "Know the Lord," for they all shall know Me, from the least of them to the greatest of them, says the Lord. For I will forgive their iniquity, and their sin I will remember no more. Jeremiah 31:34

For I will forgive their wickedness and will remember their sins no more. Hebrews 8:12

**For as high as the heavens are above the earth, so
great is his love for those who fear him; as far as
the East is from the West, so far has he removed our
transgressions from us. Psalm 103:11-12**

God forgives and He forgets. You must not hold your sin against
yourself. God has forgotten them. Once you understand that in God's
eyes you have a fresh start, *what a relief it should be!* There should be
spring in your step. Joy should be in your heart.

And you should remember the example of Ronn the next time you
find a baseball in your den.

**I, even I, am He who blots out your transgressions
for My own sake; And I will not remember your sins.
Isaiah 43:25**

Looking for Holes in the Fence

Hank and I were driving down Poplar Pike in Germantown, Tennessee, past Hugh Frank Smith's horse farm, when we encountered about 20 horses standing on the road. We stopped the truck, got out and started herding them back through the gap in the fence. At the same time, Hugh's daughter, Melanie, drove up and began to help.

As we guided the horses, cars drove within a foot of them and us, at over 40 miles an hour. We had to put a rope on some of the horses to get them back in. Thankfully, all the horses made it back into the pasture, safe and sound. It could have been a disaster for them and us.

As I thought about it later, I wondered how this might have played out from the horses' point of view.

Scene One: The Pasture

Trigger: "Hey look, there's a hole in the fence."

Flicka: "It sure is. Someone needs to get that fixed."

Trigger: "Are you kidding! This is our chance to get out of this prison!"

Chorus of horses: "That's right! Ride on!"

Flicka: "I can't believe you want to leave our beautiful meadow. And Mr. Smith loves us so much. He takes care of us, feeds us, and makes sure we stay well."

Trigger: "Is he a horse? He doesn't know what's best for us. I'm leaving."

Chorus of horses: "Hi Ho Trigger!"

Scene Two: Poplar Pike

Flicka: "This is dangerous! That car almost hit Mr. Ed. Let's go back to the pasture!"

Trigger: "No way! This is living! We're finally outside the old pen!"

Flicka: "This is not safe! It's scary! It's not where we are supposed to be!"

Trigger: "You don't know what you're talking about. He has you brainwashed."

Flicka: "We need help! We need to get out of this danger and back home!"

I don't know how well horses can communicate, but if they can, this might be how it went down. Sounds a lot like some people I know. Like me. We're often looking away from God instead of toward Him. We don't always recognize that He knows best and His commandments are for our own good. Instead, we keep looking for holes in the fence.

I want to be the one who trusts God so much that I am no longer tempted to leave. I want to be the one to encourage others to do the same. And I want to be the one to enjoy God's love and his care each day. And to look forward to even better things in the next life.

I know this analogy is not perfect. But it works for me. Horses are not the smartest animals I've cared for. Well, compared to a cow, they are Einsteins. But horses can be stubborn and mean and pretty hostile to their owner.

At the same time, they can bring their owner a lot of pleasure. A lot of times, this comes by just being obedient. Coming to the owner when called. Trotting when asked to trot. Staying in the stall. Staying in the pasture. Holding still when their shoes are worked on.

I want to bring pleasure to God. I know I don't do that nearly as much as I should. I am going to use horses to remind me about this. God's fences are there for a reason. He wants me to quit thinking about how to get into trouble. He wants me to concentrate on His plans for me.

Trust in the Lord with all your heart, and do not lean on your own understanding. Proverbs 3:5

The Only Thing Between the Wolves and You is *Me*

Some of the more adventurous episodes in my life have been the times I've spent with Ken Jenkins. Ken is what I call an adventure photographer. He has taken photos for the State Farm National Parks Calendar for over 25 years. His wildlife photography at his *Beneath the Smoke* gallery in Gatlinburg, Tennessee, is known all over the nation. Ken is the creator of Wilderness Wildlife Week, an event in January that draws thousands of wildlife enthusiasts from almost every state.

I was able to tag along with Ken on a photography trip to North Dakota, South Dakota and Wyoming. Our first stop was in the Black Hills of South Dakota. Ken was in the market for some wolf photos. A wildlife guide led us to a pack of about 12 wolves. As the wolves got closer to us, the guide produced a metal tool that looked like some type of electric cattle prod. When the wolves saw it, they backed off a little. Not far enough, for my money.

While the expert tapped the ground with his implement, Ken snapped photos of wolves in every direction. I looked around. There was no path of escape. Trying to make conversation and ease my hysteria, I said to the guide, "How much electricity is in that thing?"

The guide laughed and said, "Well, I was running a little late this morning and couldn't find the real thing. So, I just broke the head off a seven iron. But they've seen me before and a few have tasted the business end of my prod. They associate me with the results."

As I looked at the large wolves, with saliva dripping off their teeth, I said, "You mean the only thing standing between us and those wolves is that *golf club?*"

He looked at me and said, "No. The only thing standing between you and those wolves is *me.*"

Well, we made it back with our arms and legs. As I have reflected on

that adventure, I was reminded that our real guide is Jesus. He stands between us and evil. And, unlike my guide, he does have the power to protect us. He is greater than the Evil One. And He is able to guide us through the scary parts of life to our reward.

Maybe we can't always see him in the woods with us, but He tells us to have faith and courage. He is with us.

For He will command His angels concerning you to guard you in all your ways. Psalm 91:11

The Lesson of Nestle

We lost a pet last night. Nestle. Seventeen years ago, Janet heard the cries of a kitten coming from the neighbor's house. About the time they got the white kitten, they had a baby. They didn't know what to do with the little cat, so they stuck it in the storage building out back. Janet asked if she could have it. They said yes before she could finish the question.

Since then, Nestle has been queen of the house, sleeping with children, nipping at younger cats who got in her space and wanting to be wherever everyone else was. I watched her die.

It's never easy to watch a person or an animal die. It's not pretty. It's usually just the opposite. What a hole death leaves.

I hate having to say goodbye to loved ones, to friends, to beloved pets and most recently, to Nestle. She won't be the last. Then one day, I'll cause others pain when I pass away.

That's why I'm eager for us all to get to Heaven. Where there's no death. There's no heartache. There's no having to say goodbye.

I have no facts to base this on, but I hope that pets make it to Heaven. My pets loved me more than some of my family members! I want

117

them there. I just think it would make Heaven a better place to have some dogs sleeping on the porch and in the bed.

I hope there will be places to fish. I have it pictured that my father is fishing right now, with a chair set up for me. I also hope there is a place to hike over wonderful trails with beautiful scenery. Is it too much to ask for four wheelers? Well, that's on my hope list, too, because of some great memories I've had with Hank on them.

There are some wonderful old hymns that depict a place where there are no tears and no goodbyes. Here's one of my favorites:

While we walk the pilgrim pathway, Clouds will over-spread the sky.
But when traveling days are over, not a shadow, not a sigh.
When we all get to Heaven, what a day of rejoicing that will be!
When we all see Jesus, we'll sing and shout the victory.

A Wise Investment of Time

I loved being a Boy Scout. I have great pride in being able to say that I'm an Eagle Scout. Scouting helped foster my life-long love and appreciation for nature. I developed skills that I have used ever since.

The parents at my church wanted a scout troop, but none of the dads had any experience in scouting. A man at our church, E.L. Vandiveer, was a legend in the world of Boy Scouts. He was a long time scoutmaster, but had retired a few years earlier, after several decades of service.

The fathers asked for his help. They did not realize just how great a commitment it would be. But he said yes. He was much older than our dads. He knew the kind of energy it took to lead a pack of wild boys. He knew the kind of time it would take to effectively teach boys about the outdoors. There would be training and campouts and summer camp and special camps and parent training. He didn't know a single boy. He was old enough to be our grandfather. He was beginning to have some health problems. And, oh yeah, he owned a service station. But he said yes.

We worked hard to learn scouting skills – knot tying, lashing, fire starting, first aid, camping, cooking, hiking, swimming, boating, astronomy and so much more. We learned how to get along, how to show respect, how to lead, how to perform under pressure and how to enjoy life in the great outdoors.

For almost four years, I basked in the wonderful life of being a Boy Scout. And being a Boy Scout under Mr. Van. I can still see him sitting in his chair, by the campfire, laughing with us, telling us stories, listening to us, and showing us his approval.

The years went by, we grew up and went our separate ways. David became a doctor. Dennis became a newspaper editor. Jerry became the president of a utility company. We scattered and didn't stay in touch.

One day, I received a call from Mr. Van's wife. She said Mr. Van didn't have long to live. She thought the best medicine would be to hear from some of his old scouts. So, I went over to his house, sat by his bed and relived those scouting days with him. He had photos of us around the bed.

I helped send word out to his scouts. I knew some. Some I didn't.

When I told their secretaries that I was calling about Mr. Van, they all took my calls. They all called Mr. Van. He spent the last hours of his conscious life talking to his scouts. Boys who had turned into men. Men who told him what they should have told him a long time back. He had played an important role in their lives. It was time well spent. Time that would never be forgotten. Time that would be treasured.

Mr. Van is one of my heroes. He did not receive or want recognition. But he made a big difference in our lives. In my life.

He made a difference because he was willing to make an investment. He knew the cost and he was willing to pay it.

I think about Mr. Van often. I have Scouting memorabilia in my office as I write this. There is my Boy Scout canteen, my spoon, knife and fork set, my Boy Scout cap, our troop neckerchief and my Eagle medal.

I have learned at least two action steps from Mr. Van's death. One, I need to say thank you more to those in my life. I shouldn't wait. Going to a funeral shows respect. Sending flowers is thoughtful. But spending time with that person when they are alive is better.

Two, I need to invest in others. In order to truly make a difference in this world, I need to see my spot and jump in. Jump in while there's time, and make a difference. And do it with complete unselfishness, like Mr. Van.

Want to go camping? I have time.

And let us not grow weary of doing good, for in due season we will reap, if we do not give up.
Galatians 6:9

He Just Did Good

For the past several years, I have coordinated or taught a class at my church called *Peak of the Week* on Wednesday nights. We've grown from eight attendees to 80. For the first few years, someone would dutifully get the songbooks out of a cabinet and distribute them to each chair. At the end of class, the process was reversed.

Michael Semore, one of our song leaders, mentioned that it would be a lot easier if we had a library-style rolling book rack. This way, members could pick up and replace the books much easier and more efficiently. A few weeks later, a beautiful book rack appeared.

David Douglas had made that book rack. He said, "I got to looking in catalogs and found that a book case costs over $300. So I decided to make one myself, and it only cost a little over $500."

The book rack is incredibly sturdy. It's painted with non-scuff paint, and it shines with a varnish David put on it. It has revolutionized the way we distribute and collect songbooks.

When our church made the decision not to flee the city limits, as many churches did, we built a Community Life Center. We were supposed to have a kitchen, but the money ran out. So David took the shell of the kitchen and turned it into a Coffee House for the

community. He begged and borrowed tables, chairs, couches, and appliances to furnish it.

David was very active in inviting our neighbors to come over and drink a cup of coffee. The word spread that you didn't have to be a member of our church to come in and hang out. The word also spread that widows, widowers and retirees were especially welcome. David knew these folks were living by themselves, in dark houses, lonely, depressed and forgotten.

These days, it's not unusual to see a full Coffee House. Not just full of people, but of laughter and of hope. People in the community who had never darkened the door of our church are now there daily. They bring coffee cake and other treats. They bring birthday cakes and celebrate each other's birthdays. They mourn each other's losses. They use the gym for exercise. It's not unusual to see close to 100 people in the Strength and Stretch Class.

After talking to me for a short time, seeing my tears, bruises and feeling my body shake, Mother walked into the director's office and met his wife. The director's wife told Mother how little boys have a vivid imagination, and she was sure that things would get better if I stayed. Mother looked at her evenly with all the intensity of a mother bear and announced that she would be collecting my things and leaving. Then she said, "If you're not all right with that, we can take it to the ring."

I showed Mother my messy cabin, my ruined cap and the candy she had sent me - on *Gary's* bed. I showed her that Gary made a boy who wet the bed sleep on the springs. I showed her the boxing ring. She searched for Gary, too, but I guess the director's wife got to him first.

I had never been homesick. Then again, I had never been away from home longer than a day or two. It was the worst feeling in the world.

I have felt that feeling in different ways since – watching my children go off to college. Saying goodbye for the last time to my father. Burying a pet who loved me with all his heart. Trying to comfort a child who was experiencing the same thing.

Heaven on earth to me would be living with my parents and children and other loved ones, preferably on the lake. But I've learned that doesn't last.

Now I am homesick for a different home. It's a home where my father is. It's a home where there is no meanness, no tears, no fights, no disease, no divorce, no broken dreams, no selfishness, no hidden agendas and no death. It's a home that will be permanent. I hope there is a lake, but that's just me.

I have learned many great things about earth – fall weather, a loving dog, a front porch, coffee in the morning, camping, fishing, football on Saturdays, a fire in the fireplace, a meal shared together, a cabin on the lake or in the mountains, cooking over a campfire, the smell of a good steak, people who love me and so much more! But it all comes to an end. All of it.

That's why I'm homesick in a much better way these days. I'm ready to go be with my family. I'm ready to never have to say goodbye again. I'm ready to leave heartaches and death and disappointments and sickness. I'm tired of funerals. I'm tired of the horror of accidents. Sometimes, especially as I grow older and suffer one loss after another, I feel beaten up and scared about the safety of loved ones.

I'm ready for home. Jesus already took it to the ring. Jesus probably won't be coming back in a Chevrolet Bel Air, but I'm watching and waiting. How about you?

In My Father's house are many dwelling places; if it were not so, I would have told you; for I go to prepare a place for you. If I go and prepare a place for you, I will come again and receive you to Myself, that where I am, there you may be also.
John 14:2-3

I Want to Be Like Jimmy

Jimmy Moffett has been a preacher for over half a century. He is not preaching full time these days. It is my pleasure to sit by him at church and share a meal with him each week.

I enjoy watching how he lives. I think he most enjoys visiting with people – in all situations. He loves to go to church. And he makes the rounds in the sanctuary each Sunday before the service begins. He goes from person to person, saying hello, introducing himself, taking notes on who is about to go into the hospital or needs a special prayer.

He visits the hospitals weekly, praying with those who are about to have surgery and those who are on a final approach to the next life.

He visits senior citizens every week, bringing brownies or cookies. He always has a kind word and a prayer.

He is quick to visit a funeral home.

He writes many cards of encouragement each week.

And he preaches and teaches several times a month.

He studies the Bible with various men in various stages of their walk

with God.

He is not afraid to breach the awkwardness and talk to men and women about their eternal destinies.

As a Texan, he is also not afraid to wear cowboy boots, but I digress.

Jimmy's life is not pain-free. His wife passed away. He misses her every day. He misses seeing his children, who live hundreds of miles away. And yet, he fills his days with service to others.

I compare Jimmy's lifestyle to a small church I pass by on the way to fish in Arkansas. The parking spots close to building have the names of members on them. Visitors park in the back. That small church is at least 70 years old. It still meets in the original small building.

I choose the way Jimmy lives his life. He draws people to God, makes them feel good about who they are, and lets them know that he loves them.

I want to be like Jimmy.

If anyone serves me, he must follow me; and where I am, there will my servant be also. If anyone serves me, the Father will honor him. John 12:26

Service with No Recognition

Back when I was a student in college in Nashville, I had two room-mates for a couple of years. We'll call them Jay and Rodney because that was their names. We lived on the sixth floor. Another student lived at the other end of the floor. His name was Ted. Ted had severe cerebral palsy. He was confined to a motorized wheelchair. He could do very little for himself.

He needed help when he ate. He needed help getting books out of his bag that was located in the back of his chair. He needed help turning the pages. He needed help getting dressed. He needed help getting undressed, bathing, brushing his teeth and using the bathroom.

As far as I know, no one was employed to help Ted. If they were, they certainly weren't fulltime. Which brings me to the start of this story.

When Ted was ready to go to bed, he had to find someone on the sixth floor to help him. As you might imagine, this was not a popular job.

I remember one night in particular. Jay, Rodney and I were all study-ing in our little suite. That's when we heard the motor of a wheelchair. It was at the other end of the hall. It came to a stop. Then *knock . . . knock . . . knock.*

After about 30 seconds, *knock . . . knock . . . knock.* This was a few doors down. No answer.

The whirl of a motor down to the next door, *knock . . . knock . . . knock.*

After about 30 seconds, at the next door, *knock . . . knock . . . knock.*

As the motor became louder, we worked in unison to turn the lights out and maintain complete silence.

Finally, it was our turn. *Knock . . . knock . . . knock.* Followed by silence. We were the last room in the hall. That might be why we heard the ramming sound of Ted's wheelchair hitting our door. Not once, not twice, but three times.

And then, "Rodney . . . Jay . . . Steve . . . I know you're in there." This was followed by a low but audible, "heh, heh, heh." Ted's version of humor.

Finally, one of us would open the door and go with Ted to help him get ready for bed. It was a ritual we went through often.

As I think back on that time many years later, I confess that I've always been a little proud of the fact that we helped Ted. This was a fairly unpleasant job, especially for 19-year-olds. I am not proud of the fact that we had to be coerced out of the darkness.

But I mostly think about Ted. What was it like for him to have to ask? Every night! And what was it like to have to ask, knowing that no one wanted to help him? While it was unpleasant for us, I have no concept of what it must have been like for him.

College taught me a lot of things. It was eye-opening and memory making. My encounters with Ted still keep me contemplating. How should I have responded? And who do I need to focus on today? The ones who are unpleasant? Those who are not easy to listen to, not easy to be with and not overly grateful for the help?

How should I respond? And, by the way, how should you? You have your own opportunities. How are you doing?

Jesus makes it clear in passages like Matthew 25 that He is extremely interested in how we treat folks like Ted. Notice that He didn't say folks who made the most money, who lived in the largest houses, who were the most attractive, who had the best season tickets, who had the most trophies, who were members of the most boards or who had the best second homes.

He said blessed are those who were consistently kind and understanding and patient and generous with the least of these.

There will never be a shortage of people for us to help. There are many conditions in the human race that require help. Service gets tiring. It is ongoing. It is often frustrating. It is seldom recognized or rewarded. We have to encourage each other in our service. We also must remind ourselves of the importance of our service.

I need to be more intentional before I even meet people with needs. I need to know that I'm going to have to have patience. And I should not count on receiving kind words for my efforts.

But, I need to remember that the kind words I will receive will be from Jesus.

The King will reply, "Truly I tell you, whatever you did for one of the least of these brothers and sisters of mine, you did for me." Matthew 25:40

Taking My Own Advice

During the time that I taught school, I always helped with graduation responsibilities. This was because I taught seniors. As you may recall, graduation is an exciting, busy time of the year. Finals have to be taken, lockers have to be cleaned out, end of the year activities are happening right and left, relatives come into town, thank you notes have to be (or should be) written, and on it goes.

On the night of graduation, all of the seniors gathered in the library to put their caps and gowns on. At the appropriate time, they lined up and headed for the auditorium. My job was to stand at the library door and make sure ties were straight, graduation regalia was correct and caps were level. It was also a time for the seniors to give me a last hug and thank you.

On this particular graduation night, the first senior smiled at me, the second spit out her gum in the garbage can I held and the third just passed by me. One by one, the seniors walked by me with no hug, no thank you. They only stopped if I needed to adjust something for them.

Only one senior out of 100 said thank you. She gave me a hug and whispered in my ear, "Thank you for being my teacher."

I used to tell that story to point out how most people don't say thank you nearly enough. I wanted to show how we don't take advantage of our opportunities to show gratitude. I talked about some of the students who needed extra help. I talked about some of the students who had rough times during the year, and what I had done to make it better. I talked about kids whose parents had died during the year and how I spent time with them. I talked about kids whom I didn't give up on. I talked about the days I stayed late or came in early to help a student. And then pointed out that all but one just walked past me.

I thought it was a great message. In some ways, it was. I probably also enjoyed it because I got to vent. Then, it hit me. What did that say about *my* actions? I was just standing there, like a statue, *waiting* for these *kids* to demonstrate their thankfulness. When what I should have done was show my gratitude and love to them.

Twelve months later, that's exactly what I did. I hugged each one. I said a word of validation to each student. I high-fived them and took a bunch of photos with them. What a lesson I learned! I couldn't control *their* initiative, but I could certainly control mine!

I did the same thing every year after that. I had students later tell me that what I did and said meant more to them than anything they heard in the speeches that followed. Well, okay, two or three students said that.

All I know is that I felt much better about the evening. I felt much better about the fact that the students left knowing how I felt about them.

I learned that this should serve as a model for the way I show others how I feel about them. As time has passed, it's become more impor-

tant to me to *show* than to *receive* gratitude. Although I still appreciate it.

Instead of complaining about how cold and aloof a church is, I need to initiate conversations and invitations.

Instead of complaining about how I never get a card, I need to work on sending cards out regularly.

Instead of complaining that the preacher goes to visit very few in the hospital, I need to visit them.

There are many things I have no control over. But I do have control over a few things. And I need to realize what they are and get on with it.

> **Anxiety in a man's heart weighs him down, but a good word makes him glad. Proverbs 12:25**

A Little Too Close to the Street

I was mowing the front yard. I noticed that 2 year-old Hank was interested in something in the street. I stopped the mower and told him, "The street is dangerous. Do not put your foot in the street."

I went back to mowing, leaving Hank standing in the driveway, a safe 20 feet from the street. Every time I made the turn and came back in Hank's direction, I noticed he was at least a foot closer to the street. Finally, he had one foot on the curb and the other foot *over* the street.

I have thought about that for many years. It seems to me that's a great parallel for our lives. God tells us not to do something, and we don't. We just get as close to it as we can.

The problem is that when we are moving toward sin, who are we moving away from?

We cannot be in the light and in the dark at the same time. Neither can we be moving toward both at the same time. We are encouraged to choose whom we will serve and then to get on with it.

Since my kids went to Auburn, I have been made aware of a rivalry I didn't even know existed. The Auburn-Alabama choice. You cannot be fans of both, I learned. And the competition is strong for new recruits. Alabama fans are quick to tell you how many times they won the national championship. Auburn will tell you that their academic standards for students are much higher than for Alabama. Plus they don't kill trees. And on it goes.

You have to make a decision. It's not going to please everybody. But at least they know whose side you're on.

If you try to hide your allegiance, that makes you a closet fan. Nobody has respect for someone who is afraid to show his or her colors.

So, here's my question. Do your friends, business associates, and neighbors know that you're a Christian? Is it as obvious as whose team you're cheering for? If not, why?

There is always buzz about not offending.

Don't let anybody know your religious beliefs.
Keep your faith to yourself.
All roads lead to Heaven.

And that would be fine except Jesus said it's not. He said to let others know that you're following Him. Let your light shine. He said if we tell others about Him, He'll tell His Father about us.

That's about as clear as it gets. You can't sit on the fence. You can't hide your faith. Jesus said that makes you a hypocrite. He said the very idea makes Him want to throw up. That's about as strong as it gets.

You and I have to love the light. We can't hide anything. We have to go full out for God's team. He tells us that this is the only way to live.

He tells us that we have to trust Him. He tells us we will never regret it.

Move away from the street. It's dangerous.

For the wages of sin is death, but the free gift of God is eternal life in Christ Jesus our Lord. Romans 6:23

I tell you, whoever publicly acknowledges me before others, the Son of Man will also acknowledge before the angels of God. Luke 12:8

Thoughts in the Coon Dog Cemetery

I fulfilled a life-long goal not long ago. I went to the Coon Dog Cemetery.

Located close to Cherokee, Alabama, it was started in 1937 when Key Underwood buried Troop, his faithful coon dog, at the old hunting camp. It was not intended to be a cemetery, but years later, more than 200 coon dogs are buried in this location.

It's only for coon dogs. No other dogs are allowed. To be considered for burial, a dog must have documentation from three sources, including the Underwood Coon Dog Memorial Graveyard, that the dog is in fact a coon dog.

As I walked around the markers, I saw Troop's stone. I also saw monuments for Ranger, Flop, Bean, Blossom, Preacher, Felix and many others. The cemetery is in the woods. It's fitting for a coon dog cemetery to be in the middle of all those trees.

Several of the monuments have inscriptions.

Felix, a coon's worst enemy.

A joy to hunt with.

He wasn't the best, but he was the best I ever had.

Our dogs do share a lot with us. My father said that after his mother kissed him goodnight, he would open the window and invite his hound dog to sleep with him.

When Molly, our yellow Lab, had to be put to sleep, Hank insisted on being in the room with her. He said that she would not understand why he wasn't there. He held her in his arms as she took her last breath.

Have you ever wondered why God created dogs? Have you ever

wondered what happens to dogs after they die? I remember watching a *Twilight Zone* episode in which a man and his coon dog died in a hunting accident. He was denied access through the Pearly Gates of Heaven because he wanted his dog to go in with him. It turned out it was really hell. The message was that Heaven would not be Heaven without dogs.

I visualize Heaven as having lakes full of fish. So if I can see fish in Heaven, I can hope for dogs as well.

Our world is full of wonderful things to see. The Coon Dog Cemetery gives me mixed emotions. I'm sad to see the ending to such wonderful relationships between a man and his dog. But I'm happy they had them.

I won't know this side of Heaven just what happens to our beloved pets. But I don't have to wonder about what happens to those of us who are children of God. He told us very clearly that we would live with Him forever.

But when this perishable will have put on the imperishable, and this mortal will have put on immortality, then will come about the saying that is written, "Death is swallowed up in victory. O death, where is your victory? O death, where is your sting?"
I Corinthians 15:54-55

Life Is What Happens Along the Way

My best friend died. His name was Chuck Brewer. He called me *Big Steve*. I called him *Mr. Chuck*.

Chuck and I knew each other since kindergarten. We were in elementary school, junior high and high school together. We went to church camp together, where we later served as counselors and even directors. I was in his wedding.

Chuck was a great conversationalist. I never laughed so hard as when Chuck and I got together.

Chuck loved me as a brother. He hurt with me; he rejoiced with me.

One time when Chuck and I were at his family's condo in Destin, Florida, Chuck wanted to rent a jet boat. We took it into the bay. As we were going back in, Chuck said, "Let's see how fast this baby will go." As we shot under the bridge and into harbor, I heard a siren. I looked for the source on the bridge. Turns out, it wasn't above us. It was the Coast Guard, coming right at us! They boarded our little boat. Their disappointment was obvious when all they found were two bottles of water. They thought we might be drug smugglers. They let Chuck off with a warning.

When the captain told Chuck to start the boat, Chuck was so nervous that he pushed the key in too hard, and the whole key assembly just disappeared into the dashboard.

"What's the matter?" the captain demanded.

Chuck said, "It's gone."

So we were towed in by the Coast Guard to the rental boat place, in front of Harry T's restaurant and all the other eating establishments. We truly did look like captured drug smugglers, especially since the captain chose to leave his lights flashing.

Chuck loved the Smokies, Destin, golf, the Masters, coins, pizza, road trips, our church, a clean car, shined shoes, the zoo, walking and studying the Bible. He loved his big white Cadillac deVille with the fins and the red upholstery that he bought from his uncle. He loved Danny the wonder dog, Deenburg Deer Camp, Jackie Fargo and his brother Roughhouse and *Slap Your Mama* chocolate pies.

I was asked to speak at Chuck's memorial. I asked the audience, "What would Chuck want me to say?" I told them that we talked about this occasion for both of us. He said he would want others to know that despite the disappointments and frailties of his life, this is not the end of the story. Heaven is our final home, and we have to keep remembering that. Chuck said this kept things in perspective for him and allowed him to focus on others.

His encouragement for us, I think, would be to look for opportunities to encourage and to serve, whether taking someone to the doctor or just sitting with someone who needs a little company and conversation. He would say, *don't give up on yourself just because you may have made mistakes, and don't give up on others.*

Chuck's death was unexpected. I miss him every day. I am reminded of how short and fragile life is. Our lives together happened *along the way.* It wasn't when we were living on the beach. It wasn't when we had all the money we could say grace over. It wasn't when all our problems were solved.

It was everyday life. Some days, it was going for a walk in the neighborhood. Some days, it was taking someone to the doctor. Some days, it was cooking a hamburger on the grill. Some days, it was going to church. Some days, it was visiting a sick friend.

It was the journey. I will treasure that trip we took together, on our way to Heaven.

I can't wait to see Mr. Chuck again. I hope we can take a walk and catch up.

One who is righteous is a guide to his neighbor, but the way of the wicked leads them astray. Proverbs 12:26

Unexpected Opportunity

I received a phone call yesterday from Duncan Campbell. Duncan is a Sunday school teacher at my church and the campus minister at Harding Academy in Memphis.

"Steve, I have a request for you."

He wants me to speak in chapel, I thought.

"Are you going to be in town over the Christmas holidays?"

"Yes." *He may want me to teach his Sunday school class.*

"Well, my family and I are heading to Texas during Christmas week, and I was just wondering . . ."

He probably is supposed to give a talk at a youth retreat somewhere and needs me to fill in. Maybe he is supposed to give the Christmas sermon at church.

" . . . if you could lock the inside and outside doors at church every night about 10 p.m. It takes about 20 minutes to go to all three buildings."

Silence. No chapel talk. No Sunday school lesson. No sermon. No youth talk.

"Are you still there?"

I was. And I did

It was an unexpected opportunity. I went around with Duncan as he showed me which doors to check, which lights to turn off and which lights to turn on.

So, it's come to this. The locker of doors.

Later, I thought about his request. Why should I mind? Am I too good to walk around and shake doorknobs? Absolutely not.

Did Duncan need help? Yes.

Were there others he could have asked? Probably.

Why did he ask me? Not sure. Maybe because I lived pretty close to the building. Maybe because he knew I'd help him out.

Do I want to do it? No. I don't even stay up that late.

Is it convenient? Probably not.

But I'm glad he asked. It gives me an opportunity to serve. Helping him will mean more than any words I could have conjured up for a sermon, class, retreat or chapel.

I was sharing these thoughts with my friend, Jimmy Moffett, a long-time preacher in Memphis. His response was:

**Better to be a doorkeeper in the house of the Lord
than to dwell in the tents of the wicked.
Psalm 84:10**

I think that was humor. But there's wisdom in the idea. It feels good to be recognized by others. It raises our self-esteem when others praise us or give us validation by recognizing us in some public way. Public acts get immediate response. But there are a lot of services we are called upon to provide that no one will ever know about. And they don't need to. Some acts of kindness and love are better left a secret.

**Take care not to do your good deeds publicly or
before men, in order to be seen by them; otherwise
you will have no reward from your Father who is in
Heaven. Thus, whenever you give to the poor, do
not blow a trumpet before you, as the hypocrites in
the synagogues and in the streets like to do, that
they may be recognized and honored and praised
by men. Truly I tell you, they have their reward in
full already. But when you give to charity, do not
let your left hand know what your right hand is doing, so that your deeds of charity may be in secret;
and your Father who sees in secret will reward you
openly. Also when you pray, you must not be like
the hypocrites, for they love to pray standing in the**

synagogues and on the corners of the streets, that they may be seen by people. Truly I tell you, they have their reward in full already. But when you pray, go into your most private room, and, closing the door, pray to your Father, who is in secret; and your Father, who sees in secret, will reward you in the open. Matthew 6:1-6

Joy Giver

Yesterday, Brittney, Hank and I were at Newfound Gap in the Smoky Mountains. We had just taken photos and were getting back into the car as another vehicle pulled up next to us. The passenger door opened. A hand extended for me to grab. I took it and looked into the eyes of an older gentleman.

"Charlie Otis from Lancaster, Kentucky," were his first words. Still holding my hand, he looked at the snow on the trees and through the mountains. "No amount of money could create what we are enjoying right now, my friend."

He used my hand to help him get out of his SUV. His wife came around the car and said, "He's 88 years old and still enjoys life as much as ever!"

Charlie wanted to know where we were from, how long we had been there, what we had done and where we were headed. All the time, he had a smile on his face. Not a little smile. I found myself smiling back at him, larger than I usually smile.

We looked at the snow together. He commented on how it sparkled in the trees.

After he took our photo, Charlie looked back at the snowy scene and smiled even bigger, if that was possible. He said, "Goodbye Steve. It was a pleasure to meet you."

I have thought about Charlie ever since. I wish I could see him today. I wish I could spend time with him on a regular basis. He was a *joy giver*. I don't meet too many joy givers. I bet you don't, either. But I do know a few *joy robbers*. I bet you do, too. You know what I'm talking about. They suck the joy right out of an occasion. And they are good at it. They have had years to practice.

My bet is that Charlie has had years to practice, too. And he is good at it. I am glad because we need more people like Charlie.

I may never see Charlie again, but I will try to be more like him. It will take practice. I want to bring smiles and joy to others, just like Charlie did for me.

God tells us that this is the day the Lord has made and we should rejoice and be glad in it. Why? Because we are grateful for the beauty of the earth, what He did and what He's going to do. Sounds like a great reason for joy.

Your love has given me great joy and encouragement, because you, brother, have refreshed the hearts of the saints. Philemon 1:7

Remember to Change Your Oil

David LaVelle and I were in the hospital together when we were born, and we've been friends ever since.

David is an orthopedic surgeon and partner in Campbell Clinic in Memphis. He was asked to speak at the commencement service of his alma mater, The University of Tennessee at Martin. When he got up to speak, he said hello to everyone and then said:

"Okay, point number one, change your oil every 3,000 miles."

Everyone laughed. The students loved it. The parents appreciated it.

It's still a good point. Take care of what you have.

That car will last a lot longer if you keep fresh oil in it.

Your body will work better if you watch what you eat and exercise.

The beauty of David's point is that while we are looking at the big goals, we need to remember that along the way, we have to take care of the details in our lives.

We need to keep the house painted, the yard mowed, the hair cut, the dog fed, the bills paid, the tires inflated and our commitments met. I found it interesting that with all of David's achievements, his first suggestion was to keep the oil changed.

I had another friend whose daughter called him from college one day to say that she was having car trouble. She said she was driving along and the car made a terrible noise and then quit. Then smoke started coming out of the hood. The car had to be towed. She said, "Daddy, I'll let the mechanic explain it to you."

The mechanic told my friend that the engine was blown because she was driving it without oil. Turns out she had seen the oil light for some time and didn't do anything about it.

There's a big lesson here about being intentional in taking care of what God has allowed us to have. I also think about other things I need to take care of. So, let me ask you some of the questions I ask myself.

How are you taking care of your family?
Your spouse? Your children? Your grandchildren?
How about your parents? Your grandparents?
How about the older people who were good to you as you grew up?
What about that elderly neighbor?
What about others that you know who could use your help?

Maybe it means a phone call to check on them. Maybe it's a card. Maybe it's a visit. Maybe it's a hand in trimming the bushes. Or taking the kids somewhere. I don't know what it is. But you do.

I do know that the clock is ticking for you and me. We won't be on this earth long. How we take care of people and things is about all we can control. So how are you doing?

I'm going to do better. Where's that rag? I need to check the oil.

For everyone to whom much has been given, much will be required. Luke 12:48

A Lifestyle He Demands

Our church was having its annual father-son breakfast, and my father and I were asked to be the emcees.

What a Norman Rockwell occasion. It was, at least, until it began. I stood up from the head table to welcome everyone. As I did, I bumped my fresh cup of hot coffee right into Daddy's lap. He jumped up and invented a dance never seen before or since. This amazed and bewildered many of the attendees. Some did not know that hot coffee was making him move in that fashion. Others did not know he could move that fast. Others just clapped.

He was a good sport about it. After his face resumed its normal color, he sat back down. So I welcomed everyone, relieved that the worst was behind us.

I was wrong.

I asked my friend, Chris, a brown belt in karate, to give us a short demonstration. This would serve as our entertainment. A manly form of entertainment for a father-son event. Chris looked very regal in his ghee. The first thing Chris did was to produce a cinder block. I think he may have taken it from a work site. He announced that he was going to break it in half.

167

I began to feel anxiety. Chris placed the block on the floor in front of him, raised his hand, thrust his hand with great speed on the cinder block . . . and all we heard was the sickening thud of his hand on the still intact concrete. We groaned in unison.

Chris' face turned a shade similar to what Daddy's was a few minutes earlier. He announced he would try it again. Same result. I stood up and said, "Chris, we appreciate you giving this a great try. Let's all give Chris a round of –"

Chris looked at me, wild-eyed, and said, "Sit down." He gave it a third try and the thing cracked in half.

Chris then asked me to come up and hold a board that he was going to break with his foot. It was an inch thick. I don't know if you have ever held a board for someone to break with his foot. I had not. I quickly learned that a one-inch board is hard to break anyway. I also learned that to be broken, it must be held firmly. I was instructed to hold it with my arms outstretched, my legs locked. I additionally learned that a foot coming toward you at lightning speed is alarming. It did not take long to realize that this was a lot of energy being directed at a board I was holding. And it also was easy to figure out that if he broke the board, his fast moving foot might or might not split my head like a watermelon.

In retrospect, we should have practiced. If we had, I would have given the job to some kid who didn't know any better. But we didn't. So, when the foot of Chris struck the board I was holding, I bounced back, causing the board not to break. Chris gave me that wild animal look and told me to hold still. I gripped the board, closed my eyes and braced for impact. I felt the sting in my hands, heard wood splintering and awaited my fate. Fortunately I was okay. I think some in the crowd were disappointed. Perhaps my father.

The morning turned out fine. We had homemade biscuits, eggs and country ham. We committed to be better sons and fathers. I think we were. It was certainly a morning I will never forget.

I learned that sometimes things don't turn out the way you plan. Despite your best efforts, things can go South real quick. But I also learned that if you don't give up and keep a good attitude, usually things work out.

What's true for a father-son breakfast years ago is also true for you and me right now. That wasn't the last time I was surprised, embarrassed or even humiliated. I recall the words that God is greater than our problems. He asks us to trust Him even when we can't see how things can turn out.

It's a lifestyle that He demands.

You, dear children, are from God and have overcome them, because the one who is in you is greater than the one who is in the world. I John 4:4

The Lesson of the Battery

Hank and I had been fishing at a pond one Saturday morning just outside of Pleasant Hill, Mississippi. It was a beautiful day, we had fun catching fish, eating our Vienna sausage and watching the wildlife. On the return route, we had the jon boat on top of my Ford Explorer. The trolling motor was in the back. I placed the battery on the back seat.

As we unloaded the boat and motor, I noticed that the battery had bounced on its side. When I lifted it up, I saw battery acid on the seat.

By the time we stored everything, the acid had eaten through the leather, through the foam and through anything else it touched, so that I could see straight through to the floorboard. Hank and I surveyed the damage. The back seat looked like a commode.

I had to have the whole back seat replaced. I realized that I was not using a marine battery that wouldn't spill. And I should have never put the battery on the seat. But I did.

The old Explorer is long gone, but the memory remains. It occurs to me that battery acid is similar to sin. It destroys whatever it comes into contact with. Just like the battery acid did a number on my seat, sin can do a number on my life. And yours.

God tells us to keep away from sin. When we don't, we suffer. Sometimes for life. We often commit sin because we think we know better than God. *The rules of life might apply to others, but not to me.*

God's instructions are there for a purpose. He knows what's good and what's bad for us. He knows the terrible harm of disobedience.

The scary thing is that sin is far more destructive than that battery acid. But we don't have to suffer. All we have to do is listen and follow God's instructions.

For the wages of sin is death, but the gift of God is eternal life in Christ Jesus our Lord. Romans 6:23

Shooting Gallery For Sinners

I have a friend who made a mistake. It cost him a great deal.

I asked one of the members of that congregation how I could help. The man shrugged and said, "I don't know. But you know sin has its consequences."

I was stunned. Then I was horrified by what I heard. The person I was talking to was supposed to be a brother to my friend. Instead of trying to help, he was ready to pile on. He might as well have said, *This is a church where we shoot our wounded.*

It reminds me of when Jesus spent some time with a prostitute. When the church-going people began the *she's-a-sinner* talk, Jesus suggested that the person without sin throw the first rock at her.

The truth of the matter is that God wants us to get off our high horses and help those who need help. Period. We are told that the way we judge is the way we will be judged.

It's no wonder that so many churches are withering away. When we make a mistake, we need people to come by our side and help us. Because that's what people in the church are supposed to do. We are a hospital for sinners, not a shooting gallery. We build each other up.

173

We pick each other up.

My friend knows what he did was wrong. He suffers every day with the consequences. He needs compassion, not condemnation.

Unfortunately, in way too many of our churches today, we accept only those who are perfect. Then when they make a mistake, we let them know that they are out. And they get the message real quick.

In the vernacular of Ricky Ricardo, we are going to have some *'splaining to do* when we get to the Pearly Gates. Fortunately, there is still time to change. I just dropped my rock. Where's yours?

And as they continued to ask Him, He stood up and said to them, "Let him who is without sin among you be the first to throw a stone at her." John 8:7

And Others

Jimmy Moffett recalled a time he was invited to speak at the Harding University Lectureship in Searcy, Arkansas. Then he saw the brochure.

Come to Harding's Annual Lectureship! the front page read. In bold letters, it listed some of the outstanding, famous speakers who would be there. The last line read: *and others . . .*

The point, Jimmy said, is that most of us are others. And we have to be okay with that and see how much good we can do where God has put us.

Jimmy helped put it in perspective for me. He said, "Not everyone knows who you are, but God knows who you are and *who you helped*. And the ones you helped know who you are. In my book, that's good company."

Jimmy gives counsel that you and I need to hear. Jesus calls us to help others as often as we can. Even if our name is never in bold print. And leave the rest up to Him. We must not get tired of doing good.

**We will reap at the proper time if we don't give up.
Galatians 6:9**

Recognition This Side of Heaven

The Bible is full of scriptures about how the first shall be last and the last will be first. If this is true, I should have excellent seating in Heaven.

I recently received an invitation from my old college fraternity to come to a reunion. It happened to be on homecoming weekend and the anniversary of the fraternity's *Cowboy Show.* The famous musical presentation, now 40 years old, always sells out. As alumni, we could purchase special seating, a commemorative t-shirt and a meal for $50.

I immediately remembered a couple of decades back when I received an invitation to go to the Opryland Hotel for an earlier fraternity reunion. Even then, we had been out of college for longer than the current members had been alive. So, I showed up, with treasured mementos to present to the current officers. These included scrapbooks, vintage newsletters and beautiful photographs. I also had a speech prepared, knowing that I would probably be asked by the current president to say a few words on behalf of the alumni. It was a jim-dandy of a speech, filled with anecdotes and intellect, sprinkled with nostalgia and highlighted by a moving closing.

When I arrived in the Tennessee Ballroom, I noticed several hundred were in attendance. As I found our table, I discovered we were at the very back of a very large room. I was conveniently seated with all of the other alumni of my era. It would be a long walk to the microphone to make my talk.

Well, as you might have guessed, there was no talk. There was no mention of our escapades. Any "good old days" mentioned that night referred to what had happened over the last couple of years.

So, when I received this latest invitation, I had my misgivings. I emailed the presiding president. I told him of the alumni who might be coming. Many are very accomplished in their careers. I finally mentioned me, the originator of *The Cowboy Show*. The fellow who thought it up, picked out the songs, arranged the rehearsals, and selected the lead singers. The fellow who never dreamed that this would become a university tradition.

I told the president that I still had the playlist for our concert and that several of the original singers would be present. I inferred it could be a rare opportunity for the fraternity, the fans and the university.

I received an email back:

Dear Mr. Williford,

Thank you for indicating your interest in attending our reunion. We would be pleased to have you. The cost is $50.

I didn't go. I have had time to simmer – I mean, think about this transaction. The fact of the matter is that most of us just aren't going to get the kind of respect or appreciation we deserve this side of Heaven. I suppose we should live our lives as to not make a big deal out of that. Instead, we should make sure we show others respect, appreciation and gratitude.

Meanwhile, I shared this email with some of the alumni who attended the Opryland Hotel fiasco. They mentioned showing up at the next reunion in bowling shirts and orthopedic shoes carrying pocket protectors, walking sticks and maybe a box of Depends.

For everyone who exalts himself will be humbled, and he who humbles himself will be exalted. Luke 14:11

What's Your Plan?

The garage had not been organized in years. It was old and big. A lot of interesting items can accumulate in an old and big garage. A friend in midtown Memphis asked if I could "help" clean out her garage. That was code for me to do it while she didn't.

An old bicycle hung from the rafters. Petrified hoses refused to uncurl. There was old lumber, yard and bug sprays, car polish, dead plants, pots for live plants, shovels, rakes, sprinklers, hazard cones, fertilizer, a wheelbarrow, a homemade wagon, chicken wire, nails, screws, car batteries, license plates, lockers, bins and much more. My challenge was to bring order to chaos.

My plan was pretty simple. Take everything out. Clean the floor. Throw the junk away and put the rest back in a manner that allowed a car to park safely. Working the plan took two days of intense activity.

When I write a book, my plan is fairly simple. After I have researched and organized the material, I have a schedule for writing, usually three pages a day.

And when I wanted to build a house, I contracted it out, with the help of a paid advisor. I quickly learned about foundations, driveway width, framing, roofing, plumbing, septic tanks, heating and air conditioning, old brick, slate, casement windows, security systems, interior decorators and mortgage payments. Despite bad weather, the house was finished on schedule.

I believe in planning. I like to dream big and create a plan to reach the goal.

That's why I am embarrassed and surprised to admit to you that I do not have such a spiritual plan. I have not spent the same kind of time and energy to ask questions such as *What do I need to do this year spiritually?* I know my life won't last forever here on planet Earth, so what do I need to be about for the Lord?

Okay, before you start feeling too smug, do you have a plan? Maybe we're in the same boat. Oh, we may say things like:

I am going to go to church more.
I am going to read my Bible more.
I am going to listen to the sermon.

Those are good. But is that it?

I spent more time coming up with a plan for how to organize that garage than I have *ever* spent on my spiritual plans. And the garage plan wasn't that hard!

Well let me throw this into the kettle – what about God's plans for you and for me? We read in Jeremiah about His plans. We get other glimpes in Micah 6:8 and Matthew 25. So are we factoring His plan into ours?

You may be able to tell me when and how you plan to retire, when you want to get the house on the lake, how you are going to lose 20 pounds and how you're putting away money for next year's vacation. So, what about the plan for why you are here on the earth?

I was sharing a few thoughts along this line with my Wednesday night class at church. I asked how many had lives that turned out the way they had planned.

No hands were raised.

I asked them how many had planned on living in Memphis.

Two hands went up.

I asked if it was possible to follow God's plan even if you were living in conditions you weren't crazy about.

All hands went up.

After thinking about this for a while, here's what I have come up with. I need to spend some time thinking and praying about my plan for Bible study and also about my skill set. I need to ask God to use me and help me to see what He wants me to be about.

Your plan will be different from mine. In my mind, part of being God's person is to show our gratitude to Him. And the way to maximize our efforts is to create a plan.

Maybe it's raking leaves for that lady down the street.
Maybe it's writing thank you notes to those you come in contact with.

183

Maybe it's reading to that teacher who can no longer read.

Maybe it's spending time regularly with that widow or widower who is lonely.

Maybe it's starting a men's prayer group.

Maybe it's fixing that kid's bike.

Maybe it's asking the neighbors to come over for coffee, donuts and reading the Bible.

Maybe it's inviting friends, relatives and neighbors to church.

Maybe it's inviting more people over to the house.

Maybe it's sharing a fishing trip.

You and I need to create a plan. Then we need to build the activities into our schedules. We must do this to maximize our time here on earth.

"For I know the plans I have for you," declares the Lord, "Plans to prosper you and not to harm you, plans to give you hope and a future."
Jeremiah 29:11

Validation

I've mentioned that I was a school teacher at one point in my life. It started with me substituting for an ill Speech teacher. I ended up teaching Speech for eight years. It was an eye opening experience.

For example, teachers were supposed to stand outside their doors during class changes. I remember standing by my door during those first few days. I said hello to every student who passed by. I might as well have been a plant. They weren't used to acknowledging teachers.

As I walked through the hallways, I noticed the same phenomenon. Students didn't say hello to me. And, to my greater surprise, some of the teachers did not say hello. They had been conditioned to be unfriendly!

So, I began validation lessons in my Speech class. The first lesson was simple:

Say hello.

The second lesson was also simple:

Say hello back.

From there, we moved on to the advanced stuff, like:

Smile when you see others.
Ask questions during a conversation.
Compliment others.
Hold the door for others.

This was an unfamiliar paradigm to these high school students. They said they had used validation in first grade, but not after that.

One year, I gave extra credit to any student who could say hello to me before I said hello to them. As I sat at the teachers' table at lunch or walked down the halls, other teachers were amazed at my popularity. I never told them about the extra credit.

As the year progressed, we moved on to other skills like writing thank you notes. Many of the students did not know how to address an envelope! This was a prestigious, college-prep high school. Most of the kids received academic scholarships. How was this skill left behind?

So, we wrote thank you notes. The results were amazing. The recipients wrote back, saying they would frame the cards and keep them forever.

One day, when the students walked in, I placed blank sheets of paper on everyone's desk. I told them to write their name at the top. "Now, everyone get up, and write something to validate each one of your classmates. And sign your name." They did. Many spent several minutes on each validation. The kids kept their validation sheets - some taped them in their lockers or put them on their bulletin boards at home. They would later say that this was one of the best days of class.

They were truly validated by their classmates.

We talked about the power of validation. They understood that the more they interacted with and made a difference in the lives of each other, the stronger their validation would be the next time we did this exercise.

A few weeks later, we had a Valentine's party. Except we called it a Validation Party. Everyone made Validation Boxes from shoe boxes. Each student received a validation card from every other student in the class. It was like primary school. Except I asked them to write notes of validation on the cards. They walked around and placed their cards in each other's boxes. It was a fun day and the students remembered the power of validation for the rest of the year.

Of course, other teachers heard about the validation exercises. A few were critical and cynical about just what went on in Speech class. So,

I decided that we needed to validate the teachers. I placed the teachers' names in a Tupperware container. They were randomly selected by student validation teams. These teams would validate their chosen teacher for a week.

The first thing they had to do was to interview their teacher. They found out where the teacher grew up. They found out about the teacher's family. They found out about the teacher's favorite activities and foods and sports teams.

At the beginning, many of the teachers were reluctant to participate. They smelled a trick of some kind. The head of one department simply refused. Fortunately everyone else agreed to participate.

Then the fun started! The students began to validate the teachers. Take the coach and guidance counselor who were newly married. The students arranged a private luncheon for them in a conference room at school. Then there was the teacher who was about to have a baby. The students arranged a baby shower.

Or take the math and science teachers who had been married for several years. The students learned that they met right there at school and their first date was to a soccer game at school. The validation team helped them relive their first date. They reserved two seats at the soccer game, gave them a gift certificate for the restaurant they went to years ago and even presented them with flowers.

Another team discovered that their teacher loved a particular hymn. They convinced chorus members to come to the teacher's classroom and surprise her with the song.

Teachers received candy, cakes, Mexican food, homemade ice cream, grilled hamburgers, pizzas, fruit, framed photos, car washes, sports memorabilia, scrapbooks, CDs of their favorite music, babysitting, wood carvings, gift baskets, breakfast, Starbucks coffee, donuts, hand-made pottery and even big signs in front of the school.

The teachers got it. Even the skeptical found that it feels good to be validated. Of course, the lesson for you and me is that this doesn't have to be a school project. It's what we need to be about every day. Plus, it's fun.

Therefore encourage one another and build each other up, just as in fact you are doing.
I Thessalonians 5:11

It's Time to Fly Away

There is a cardinal that I see every day. He spends most of his time in front of my next door neighbor's sun porch. In particular, he spends most of his time in front of the big windows. They have a mirror effect. He can see his reflection. He thinks it is another bird, and he attacks the image with a fury. He bangs into the window with his beak, with his claws and sometimes with his body.

All day long he attacks. Day in and day out, he attacks. All year long, he attacks. This is the second year that I've kept up.

You'd think that sooner or later, he'd figure it out. You'd think that he would catch on that this strategy isn't successful. You'd think he might reassess his actions and their results. You'd think he might try something different. You'd think he might decide, on maybe day 587, it was time to move on to Plan B.

It's time to fly away.

Yet, as sure as the sun comes up, Mr. Cardinal is spending all of his energy on his phantom nemesis. It consumes his entire existence.

Are you banging against a window, attacking something that really isn't there? Maybe you can't forgive yourself for something that happened a long time ago. You've asked God for forgiveness, but you just can't let it go. God tells us that He not only forgives, but also forgets our sins.

It's time to fly away.

Or maybe someone hurt you, and you can't forgive him or her. You might not just be hurt, but mad. You've told everybody who will listen about this transgression. You've slung hate and mud and vile. But you still feel bad.

It's time to fly away.

Or maybe you're mad at God. Some terrible things have happened to you, and you blame God. How could a good God allow such unspeakable nightmares to occur in your life? You have shut Him out of your life. You have vocalized your anger to Him in public and private. You have vowed never to have anything to do with Him again. Meanwhile, there's still pain and heartbreak in your life. Maybe it's time to consider that He didn't cause it, but He can help you get through it.

It's time to fly away.

God has given you and me the gift of another day. We can use it any way we want. But what good is it to do the thing that's not working over and over? There is much good to be done.

It's time to fly away.

Brothers, I do not consider that I have made it my

own. But one thing I do: forgetting what lies behind and straining forward to what lies ahead, I press on toward the goal for the prize of the upward call of God in Christ Jesus. Phillipians 3:13-14

Where It's Wonderful and Permanent

When David Douglas was in the final stages of his life, a friend of mine said, "Did you ask him to say hello to your father?" I didn't, and I've been thinking about that. I should have.

I have an image of Heaven that has my father doing one of his favorite things. Fishing on the side of a lake. Sitting in one of those vintage outdoor chairs with strips of cloth crisscrossing the frame. He has the old Zebco rod and reel on his lap, his legs are crossed, he's wearing a cap and watching his float. There's a vacant chair for me. Waiting.

Years ago, we were at our farm. When I walked down the drive by the garage, Hank was waiting for me, sitting on his Honda Ranger 4-wheeler. Ready to take a trip through the woods. I thought, *I hope Heaven is like this. Waiting for the ones we love to ride a 4-wheeler through the woods.*

I don't know what Heaven is going to be like or look like. But I know it won't disappoint us. I know it is something that we can and should look forward to. And I know that it is better than here.

I enjoy life. I enjoy the changing of the leaves. The snow on the ground. A cardinal in a pine tree. A deer jumping over a fence. A great hamburger. A Christmas trip to the mountains. Fishing on a calm lake as the sun comes up. A walk through the woods. A great SEC football game. A campfire. A steak on the grill. A good Eagles' song.

But I also *don't* enjoy life sometimes. Heartache. Divorce. Selfishness. Stress. Worry. Cancer. Broken bones. Death.

Aren't you glad to know what's painful here on earth is temporary, and what's wonderful in Heaven is permanent? Spread the word!

I will rejoice over Jerusalem and take delight in my people; the sound of weeping and of crying will be heard in it no more. Isaiah 65:19

A Life of Abundance Each Day

At a very early age, Hank started fishing with me on Saturday mornings. Hank was probably about 5. We began going to a little pond on a farm outside of Victoria, Mississippi.

We usually sat on the bank and caught several brim and an occasional bass. We ate Vienna sausages and crackers. We explored the pond's perimeter for tadpoles, frogs, minnows, crickets and anything else that caught our eye.

From that beginning, we fished in many ponds and lakes. We caught rock fish in South Dakota, fought off water moccasins as we fished on the Cache River in Arkansas, learned how to trout fish on the Little Red River a little farther west in Arkansas and fished for bass and catfish on the Tennessee River.

Our first boat was a jon boat that we keep beside Hank's pond in northern Mississippi. Hank's next boat was a Bass Tracker. After we learned how to back the trailer into the water without embarrassing ourselves, we then learned how to maneuver the boat back onto the trailer in swift water.

For the last several years, Hank and I have enjoyed many adventures in that boat. We have traveled miles up and down the river. We've enjoyed meals on little islands, waited out storms under umbrellas, watched Fourth of July fireworks many times from the boat and pulled in a lot of fish.

Hank is now in college. Saturdays aren't the same. The jon boat doesn't go in the water too much anymore. The Bass Tracker sits under cover, collecting dust. When Hank is home, he is busy with other things. Our time is limited.

As I think back on our many adventures and memories, it seems like a perfect parallel to life. We work hard and plan our futures, only to find that what happened along the way was just as much fun, if not more, than now.

God calls us to a life of abundance every day. Life is not about what happens at the end of our rainbow. Sometimes we don't live long enough to experience the second homes or a life of retirement. As we work towards our goals, we must enjoy the journey. We are *called* to enjoy it. We cannot get so busy with tomorrow that we fail to enjoy today's little pleasures.

There were people in your life who are now gone. You would give anything to have one more day with them. That's how I feel about those days on the river with Hank.

While you and I can treasure memories of days gone by, we cannot live in the past.

What I can do in the days that I have left is to not take this day for granted. It won't be everything I want it to be, but it is today. It is the day that the Lord has made. I will be glad in it.

The thief cometh not, but for to steal, and to kill,
and to destroy: I am come that they might have life,
and that they might have it more abundantly.
John 10:10

Mike Snider

Several years ago, I received a call from Mike Snider, asking if he could come talk to me. His agent had told him about me. That's why he was sitting in my office. He asked if I minded if he spit while we talked.

I told him I didn't mind his spitting into the cup, but I would appreciate it if he didn't whittle on my window sill any more. I had just paid for library paneling and new wood windows, one of which now had wood shavings beside it.

So, he put up his knife, picked up his cup and proceeded to tell me his story. He was from Gleason, Tennessee, and was a farmer with his father. They raised corn and over 1,000 hogs. Mike had also won the National Banjo Championship.

"I don't know what it is, Steve," he drawled, "but whenever I begin to talk, people just laugh."

Mike had appeared on a show hosted by Ralph Emery called *Nashville Now*. This was the *Tonight Show* of country music. Mike showed me video of his appearances on the show. The songs he played on the banjo were intricate, lively and melodic. But it was his comments before and after the songs that caused so much audience reaction. Ralph Emery would ask Mike a question and then laugh so hard at Mike's answer that he could barely breathe.

Mike wanted me to help him. So, I made the trip to Gleason. Sweet-ie, his wife was working at the "lawnmower factory." His mother was making lunch for the farmers in the back of a grocery store. Mike played the banjo for me for the first time. "I had to vacuum out the corn husks last night," he said as he opened the case.

I also saw the house that Mike was renting. One of the rooms was closed off. Mike said, "Look at this."

He opened the door. It was filled, floor to ceiling with garbage sacks. "Those are the letters that folks send me after I'm on Ralph's show." Mike said. Turned out to be thousands of letters. We loaded them up in my Ford Explorer and Mike's truck and brought them back to Memphis. We put the names in my computer and sent out a card to each person who had written:

Dear Mrs. Smith,

Thank you so much for writing to me. I just wanted you to know that I have an album out. Right now it's out in the Smokehouse, but if you'll send me ten dollars, Sweetie will slap a stamp on an envelope and send it right to you.

Love,

Mike Snider

Mike soon made more from the record proceeds than he had the whole year before.

Mike had been on the Grand Ole Opry a few times. As a matter of fact, his first time, his whole town of Gleason was invited. And they came! They loaded on buses and made the trip to Nashville. Roy Acuff introduced Mike that night.

Folks began to ask Mike to come play for their organizations, and Mike asked me if I could help him with his show presentation. We needed an auditorium to practice in. I knew we could use my church auditorium. Mike brought his banjo, and I invited my friend Bill Linder to be the audience.

There were only two microphones in the auditorium and they were stationary. One was in the pulpit. The other was at the communion table. So, that's where Mike practiced his show.

As Mike was rehearsing, Willie Mae Moore, one of the church custodians, walked in and ran out, telling anyone who would listen that a crazy person was in the sanctuary, playing a banjo at the communion table.

Mike eventually became a member of the Grand Ole Opry. If you are ever at a show, the chances are good that you will see Mike and his band.

Things have changed a little since I first saw Mike. He now has his own house and planes. He mowed down a cornfield to make a runway. He is a pilot. He has played with some of the greats in country music and is on a first name basis with most of them.

Some people thought Mike didn't really talk with that kind of accent or raise pigs or corn. They thought it was all an act. I would invite those people to spend a day in Gleason. They'd see it is no act.

I love that transparency in Mike. He is who he is. He makes no pretense and no apology.

I want to be that way, too. I want to be the best I can be. I want to be transparent. I want to reach out to others and fully understand that not everyone will care for who I am or what I'm trying to do. There's nothing I can do about that. There are some people I will never please or connect with. I just have to work hard at my profession and my walk with God.

And oh yeah, if you are ever at the Grand Ole Opry when Mike is playing, ask him to play the *TV Satellite Blues.*

For our boast is this, the testimony of our conscience, that we behaved in the world with simplicity and godly sincerity, not by earthly wisdom but by the grace of God, and supremely so toward you.
I Corinthians 1:12

Where's the First Hole and What's the Course Record?

Jerry Escue was president of Jackson Christian School in Jackson, Tennessee, when he was informed that a student wanted to be on the golf team. The only trouble - there was no golf team.

Being a former coach, Jerry decided to start and coach the golf team of one. His team consisted of one ninth grader who was new to the game. When Jerry took him out to practice, it was apparent the kid needed a lot of work.

A local tournament happened to be right around the corner. Jerry observed his young golfer tote a bag of not too many clubs right up to a tournament official and say,

"I have two questions: Where's the first hole and what's the course record?"

That's confidence. I John 5:14-15 says:

> **And this is the confidence that we have in him, that, if we ask any thing according to his will, he hears**

> **us. And if we know that he hears us, whatsoever
> we ask, we know that we have the petitions that we
> desired of him.**

So, here's my question. What is your confidence level in God's promises?

He promises to hear our prayers and answer them (I John 5:14-15).
He promises to be with us in our times of distress (Psalm 34:18).
He promises that His children can know they are saved (I John 5:13).

That freshman was a little naïve, but I admire his attitude. We may not know everything about God's nature, but we can be confident that He is with us, He loves us, He laughs and cries with us and He wants to spend eternity with us.

That's enough.

> **I write these things to you who believe in the name
> of the Son of God so that you may know that you
> have eternal life. I John 5:13**

Feeling Important

I found myself as an extra for the movie, *The Firm*. I was a last minute replacement, playing the part of a lawyer. The scene was a tax seminar in Washington. Tom Cruise was to open his seminar booklet, only to find a note from an FBI agent, played by Ed Harris.

The scene was filmed at the Omni Hotel in Memphis, Tennessee. There were at least 50 extras in the scene. Many of them were real lawyers. The director, Sydney Pollack, reminded us not to look at the camera or do anything goofy. I thought that was interesting, since we were supposed to be lawyers.

The 17-year-olds running around with head sets on were called assistant directors. They reminded me of the kids who took orders at the drive-up window at Burger King. There was a hush in the room as Tom walked in. As he walked down the aisle, I could hear people gasp. I could see women suck in their stomachs and sit up straight.

He stopped at my row and sat down a few seats away from me. He looked in my direction, and I said, "Hello Tom. Welcome to Memphis!" He smiled and gave me a half wave. It could have been short hand for, "Thanks co-actor. I'm enjoying my stay. Your welcome and courtesy are appreciated. Break a leg!" Or it could have just been a half wave.

That was the end of our relationship.

I attended a fund raising dinner where the speaker was Phil Robertson, from *Duck Dynasty* I went up to say hello before dinner. Miss Kay was extremely friendly. She came out from around the table and had her picture taken with me. Phil chose to lean back in the chair. I introduced myself, thanked him for his courage to speak up for Christianity, and welcomed him to Memphis. He looked at me through his sunglasses and gave me his thumb's up. It could have been short for, "Thank you, Steve, for coming up and saying hello. You didn't have to do that. You have made me feel welcome. Why don't you sit down and let's visit." Or it could have just been a thumb's up.

At times, we all get the message that we aren't as important as someone else.

When I read the story Jesus told in Luke 10 about a guy from Samaria who helped someone, I have questions. Where was this Samaritan going? What was his life like? Did he have his own problems? Why did he stop and help?

My bet is that *you* have been a good Samaritan in your life. Chances are, no one ever knew about it but God and that other person. And no one gave you a trophy. No one recognized your efforts. No one engraved your name on a plaque. You were not asked to make a movie about it or sit at the head table and speak about it. You did not do a good deed for the good will of others. You did it because you were at the right time and place.

And sometimes it even backfires. Ever heard this one? *No good deed goes unpunished.*

I taught a junior high Sunday school class for many years. One Thanksgiving, we wanted to do something special for a poor family in our neighborhood. The students and I collected our money, went to the grocery, bought the food and took it to them. Except they weren't at home.

A sweet old lady came from next door and hugged the kids and told them how proud she was of them. She said just leave the food with her and she'd give it to the family when they came home. She never got around to parting with that turkey.

Well, that's going to happen, and I guess we just have to learn from our (my) naivety and act smarter. But there's another piece to the puzzle.

God loves us whether we get the PR or not. God loves you, period. He loves us so much that He sent His son that He loved with all His heart to painfully clean up a mess we couldn't clean up. He didn't just do that for the rich and famous. He did it for you and me.

I was at a men's prayer breakfast early this morning and heard Lyle Hendrix say, "True worship comes when we realize what God has done for us." Once you understand that kind of love, then and only then can you really love yourself. And only when you realize your worth are you able to be a good Samaritan to others.

It might be keeping someone's kids for an afternoon. Maybe it's mowing someone's yard. Or slipping someone a few dollars. Or inviting a family over for burgers. Or maybe it's teaching that kid how to fish. Or maybe it's cleaning the commode or washing some clothes or fixing a window or holding the hand of someone who is facing the end.

God tells us in Jeremiah that He has plans for us. I don't know what that plan is, but I do know that it includes loving God, loving others and loving ourselves.

> **That the man of God may be competent, equipped for every good work. II Timothy 3:17**

How to Make Memories

Ever since I can remember, I have loved to camp. I slept outside in the backyard, on the porch, on Kenny Elliott's patio - wherever I could to see the moon and stars.

As I got older, I joined the Cub Scouts. Then the Boy Scouts. That's where camping truly started for me. We went on a lot of camping trips, in all seasons and all types of weather.

I received my Eagle Scout Award when I was 16. I have continued to camp, first by myself all over the country, and then with anyone who would accompany me. I have backpacked in the Rockies and the Smokies. And I have camped many times with Hank.

I love sharing the joy of sitting around the campfire with Hank. He learned from me how to build a fire, set up a tent, create a latrine, cook over a fire, identify snakes and poisonous plants and tie a few knots.

We have sneaked a portable TV into our campsite to watch important football games. We have transported ourselves to our campsites with 4-wheelers, ATVs and boats. We have endured rainstorms. We have listened to weather radios and coyotes at the same time.

Hank and I started early in the traditional things for boys like sports and Cub Scouts. I assisted with all those activities. But as he got older, he enjoyed the activities in nature more than he enjoyed sports. Further, he determined that while Cub Scouts was good for some, he got more bang for his buck by being with old Eagle Scout dad.

So we charted our own course. And we made memories. If you're a young dad, listen up. I can't really remember too much about my business trips during those years. I can't tell you about the meetings. They were okay, and I am grateful for the livelihood.

But what I am truly grateful for are the memories!

Hank is grown now, but he still remembers our camping trips. And guess what? He still enjoys camping with me! It's a time when we get away from everything and just enjoy our time together. Maybe he realizes it won't always be there. I don't know. I hope it's not only providing memories, but also a base for how to live.

I'm not suggesting you learn how to camp. I am suggesting you decide to make as many memories as you can with those important people in your life, and for as long as you can.

Oh, one more thing. Just because your children are grown doesn't mean you can't continue to make memories.

> **I thank my God in all my remembrance of you, always in every prayer of mine for you all making my prayer with joy, because of your partnership in the gospel from the first day until now.**
> **Philippians 2:3-5**

Simple Pleasures

I have a tradition with my children. Every Christmas season, we go to the Smoky Mountains. We do many of the same activities each year – ride the chair lift, look at the wildlife in Cades Cove, eat at the same restaurants and watch Christmas movies in the cabin.

Brittney often cooks some Christmas food. Hank and I sometimes take a hike through the mountains. We drive around and enjoy the Christmas decorations. We do some Christmas shopping. And we

laugh a lot.

I really look forward to our time in the mountains. I am grateful that Brittney and Hank still want to go. I am always sad to leave.

In my mind, this is a slice of Heaven. This is what Heaven must be like. To be with God and those you love. But in Heaven, you never have to leave. You never have to worry. You never get bad news. There is nothing to dread. There is no horror. Or fear. There is no end.

That's why death is not as bad as it looks from this side of it. It is our portal to Heaven. Where every day is the best day of your life.

If you and I can have that kind of vision, then death loses some of its sting.

As good as those trips to the mountains are, they are not perfect. There's traffic. And scary weather. And angry people. And one day, we won't be going back. Hank will have his own family. Brittney will be taking care of her own children. I will be in The Home.

Right now, life may be great for you. There may be many things you are enjoying. You just have to believe it pales in comparison to Heaven. It's a little teaser of what Heaven will be like. Plus, life here doesn't last forever.

No matter what your life is like, no matter what you have gone through or are going through, there's a better life coming! Let's work on encouraging others on our way home.

Therefore encourage one another and build each
other up, just as in fact you are doing.
I Thessalonians 5:11

Awkward Isn't Always a Bad Thing

When I was in college at David Lipscomb, I really wanted to go out with a beautiful coed named Lulu. The only problem was that she didn't know me, and I barely knew her. I was in the Student Center one day and told my friend, Ron Cherry, "You see that girl over there? I'd really like to meet her! All I know is that her name is Lulu."

"Follow me, bro," Ron replied.

I'm not sure why I trusted Ron. He had played a few tricks on me already in our fraternity. I never called him Ron anyway - His name at that time was Chop. He is a doctor now. He probably goes by Dr. Ron. Dr. Chop might be bad for business.

So, I found myself following Chop over to see Lulu. In retrospect, she probably preferred Karen.

"Lulu? Hi, I'd like to introduce my friend here."

Chop didn't even know her!

"He just got out of reform school, and he's dying to meet you. You kids have fun." And he walked away. Lulu stood there for a minute, obviously underwhelmed. We said hello to each other and then she walked away, like Chop had.

For some reason, I remained optimistic. I called her up and asked her out to a movie.

No.

I tried to analyze this. Perhaps she just didn't like movies.

So, I decided to ask her to a ballgame on campus.

No.

I tried to analyze this. Perhaps in addition to not liking movies, she didn't like basketball. By this time, my fellow students had heard about Lulu's disinterest in me. So, they encouraged me to ask her out again. After I had evaluated the two previous rejections, I decided I would ask her one last time. I don't know why. All I had to lose was any reputation and dignity I still had left.

I decided to ask her to the Tuesday night devotional, held in the middle of campus every Tuesday night. It was led by Dean Mack Wayne Craig and lasted about 20 minutes. She could just meet me there, and wouldn't even have to talk since we would be singing. And we could walk away in an opposite direction afterwards. She could even invite her sister.

I was going to ask her on Monday night. Guys on our sixth floor of the dorm started drifting into our room. They didn't want to miss the big event. More people filed in. Money didn't exchange hands, but opinions were rendered. By the time I picked up the phone, we had at least 30 guys in our room.

I picked up the phone. The room got quiet, and I posed the proposition to Lulu. I thought there was no way she could say no.

No.

When I repeated her answer, the room erupted. I thanked her and hung up.

Well, that would be reason enough for most guys to join a monastery where you took a vow of silence for seven years. However, our fraternity's banquet was coming up, and I needed a date. So, I asked Lulu. Just kidding.

I asked the girl of my dreams, Beth Horn, to go with me. Beth was beautiful, charming, popular and talented. Nevertheless, I asked her if she would like to go with me to the banquet.

Yes.

I could not believe it! It was a wonderful evening, and she could not have been sweeter. We had a great time and remained friends throughout college.

In the course of the evening I thanked her for going out with me and told her what a wonderful time I was having. I couldn't help but ask, "Beth, how come you agreed to go with me and not some of these other guys?"

She smiled and said, "Because you asked."

I have thought about that for decades. A lot of guy were smarter, better looking and more suave and debonair than me. But they assumed Beth already had a date. Or they didn't want to set themselves up for rejection. Or they were intimidated by her popularity, looks and personality.

My experience with Lulu could have made me afraid to ever ask another female out on a date. I could have made up all kinds of excuses. And they would have been legitimate. But I asked. That taught me a lot. You never know if you don't ask. It's true in relationships. It's true in business. And, I can't believe that I didn't fully realize this, it's true in spiritual matters.

I have to *ask* someone about his or her spiritual condition. It's awkward, but just because something's awkward doesn't mean it's bad. It's just awkward. Asking Lulu was awkward and didn't turn out so well. It was also on the stupid side. Asking Beth was awkward until she said yes. Then it was anything but awkward.

Sometimes it's seeing that a person appears upset and simply asking, *Is everything okay?* It's amazing how that question leads to matters of the heart and soul.

Sooner or later, I need to turn to my neighbor and ask him how things are going. And I need to be willing to offer assistance. And then not be afraid to tell him how God has provided us with a way to live with Him for eternity, despite how crummy our transgressions have been here. That's the only way the lost become saved – God working through us.

The word of the day – *ask*. And, goodnight Beth Horn, wherever you are.

No man shall be able to stand before you all the days of your life. Just as I was with Moses, so I will be with you. I will not leave you or forsake you. Be strong and courageous, for you shall cause this people to inherit the land that I swore to their fathers to give them. Joshua 1:5-6

STEPHEN DOUGLAS WILLIFORD

Leonard's Vacation

I have mentioned my friend Chuck. He developed a special friendship with several men, including Leonard. Leonard lives in a small house over by the Liberty Bowl stadium in Memphis with several members of his family. Leonard worked on the railroad in years past and had lived a hard life. Chuck had been an executive with a large corporation.

One day Chuck said something about a family vacation, and Leonard said, "Excuse me, Chuck. You keep talking about these vacations that you and your family go on. What is a vacation?"

Chuck learned that Leonard had never been on anything that remotely resembled a vacation.

"I'm taking Leonard on vacation," Chuck informed me. He booked a cabin near Chickasaw State Park in West Tennessee, loaded the car up with groceries and took Leonard on the first vacation of his life.

Chuck cooked bacon and eggs each morning, fixed sandwiches for lunch and grilled steaks at night. Each evening, they sat on the porch and listened to the crickets while gazing at the stars and talking about life.

223

Leonard liked it so much he suggested that they go on a vacation once a month.

I would not wish Leonard's life on anyone. And yet, because of his past, Leonard appreciated this little vacation more than most people would.

When life is good, it's easy to forget that it won't last. But it won't. So, we have to live with that in mind. Leonard knew that, which is why he enjoyed those days so much.

How then should we live? This question was asked thousands of years ago:

"As surely as I live," declares the Sovereign Lord, "I take no pleasure in the death of the wicked, but rather that they turn from their ways and live. Turn! Turn from your evil ways!" Ezekial 33:11

We understand what turning from evil means. But what does *live* mean?

Could it mean to take advantage of the time we have, knowing that it is finite?

In his final years, Chuck was very intentional in living. For example, every week he took Leonard to the doctor. Sometimes several times a week. He took Leonard out to eat. He took Leonard to the pharmacy. He helped Leonard sort out his pills for the next day. He did the same thing for Milton.

Chuck also taught a weekly GED class in our community. He read his Bible every day. He attended weekly Bible studies and sat next to me in Sunday school. He was quick to reach out to those who needed a little money or a friendly ear or a ride somewhere.

Chuck did not know he was about to die. Far from it. He talked with great fondness about what he was looking forward to. He wanted a condo in Destin, Florida. He wanted to play golf and walk on the beach. He didn't die with a condo in Florida, but he did die in the middle of good works. Chuck's life was full of pain, but he chose to live despite the heartaches and hardships.

At Chuck's funeral, Leonard led the closing prayer. With tears flowing, he thanked God *for my friend Chuck Brewer. A good man. A man who loved me. A man I want to be like. A man who lived for Jesus.*

That's what it means to live.

One who has unreliable friends soon comes to ruin, but there is a friend who sticks closer than a brother. Proverbs 18:24

STEPHEN DOUGLAS WILLIFORD

I Think You'd Like George

We were in Gatlinburg for a convention at the Park Vista Hotel. Actually, it was my wife's convention. So, after she went to her meeting, I wandered down to the lobby. I noticed a bellman. He was standing a few feet from the front door. He said hello to newcomers and said goodbye to those leaving.

He greeted me and asked how I was doing. Well, the Smoky Mountains are my favorite place to be and I had absolutely no responsibilities for the day so I was doing great. And I told him I was doing great. I introduced myself and asked him how he was doing.

"I'm George Jenkins, and I'm excited!" he said. "I'm excited to do my job every day, but I'm especially excited today."

He handed me the second section of the local newspaper that had a full page spread on him. He had won a very select award from Hilton Hotels for outstanding customer service. There was one story after another of how George went above and beyond the call of duty.

So, I went over to the front desk for a copy of the paper. I read that George was always available to help in any capacity at the hotel. He helped wash dishes in the kitchen. He helped serve tables at conventions.

I turned to the folks behind the front desk counter and asked them what they thought about the article.

"Couldn't have gone to a more deserving employee," one employee beamed. "George is truly unselfish. He wants to help his fellow employees. He wants guests to have a great experience."

Another employee said, "When the snow came yesterday, a guest was afraid to drive up the steep road to our hotel. Word got to George who somehow made his way down the hill and told the guest that he could not drive her car due to hotel regulations, but if she would fol-

low him with her car, he would walk with her the whole way up, which was about a half mile in frigid temperatures."

I was impressed. I became more impressed. When we checked in, we were assigned a room on the third floor. My wife asked if there was a possibility of moving to a higher floor so we could see the beautiful snow on the mountains. She was told to check back that evening. So, after a meal and some shopping, we checked back. The front desk clerk said that our luggage had already been moved!

Sure enough, when we walked into a room with a view, there was our luggage and toiletries, with a note:

> Happy to be of service. If you need anything else, here's my phone number.
>
> George Jenkins

It just so happened that we saw George in the parking lot the night before we left. It was dark, and George was just leaving. I called him over and told him how much I appreciated his commitment to service.

He broke into a huge smile and thanked me and invited us to come back to the hotel. He shook our hands and disappeared into the parking lot.

Notice what George didn't do. He didn't complain about his pay. He didn't complain about working conditions. He didn't hold his hand out for a tip. He just did his job. George was no spring chicken. I don't think his goal in life was to become a bellman.

But George developed a passion for what he did.

Remember the passage in Ecclesiastes 9?

Whatever your hand finds to do, do it with all your might.

Or from Colossians 3?

Whatever you do, do your work heartily, as for the Lord rather than for men.

Your life may not have turned out how you thought. Life has a way of doing that. Maybe your career path is far different from how you envisioned it. Maybe your house or location or family situation is not how you thought it would be. Maybe others are held up as a success, and your name is never mentioned.

It's at those times that you need to think about passages from the Bible that encourage us to use our time wisely. You can't go back and undo what's been done. But you can use today in a way that makes God proud.

And, by the way, remember that what the world calls success is not always what God calls success. Think of the story of the rich man and Lazarus. When they died, the rich man went to torment and Lazarus - the beggar who sat in front of his fence - went to paradise. Over and over again, Jesus pointed out quiet, unnoticed heroes. A Samaritan who took time to help someone in need. Those who took care of the poor, the imprisoned, the helpless.

Even though I'm a great believer in following your dream, I'm also realistic enough to understand that everyone cannot achieve his or her passion. We all can't be professional athletes. We all can't be gifted musicians. We all can't be doctors. We all can't be television personalities. We all can't be homecoming queens. We all can't be quarterback of the football team, president of the senior class and Joseph in the Christmas play. What does that mean? It means *be passionate about what you can do.*

How do we stand out in our society? One way is to do our best at whatever we do.

Martin Luther King said: "If a man is called to be a street sweeper, he should sweep streets even as Michelangelo painted, or Beethoven composed music, or Shakespeare wrote poetry. He should sweep streets so well that all the hosts of Heaven and earth will pause to say, 'Here lived street sweeper who did his job well.'"

• • •

I was helping the CEO of Methodist Hospitals, Maurice Elliott, compose a speech about quality. I asked Maurice who came to his mind when he thought about quality in the health care system. He mentioned a name. I wasn't familiar with the name.

"What is his specialty?" I asked.

"Floors," Maurice said.

"He takes care of our floors. He makes sure our floors are clean and polished. I will put our floors up against anybody's floors."

I thought about that. I had to. I was shocked. In that hospital system, there were health care professionals known all over the world for their medical contributions. But who did Maurice think of first when he thought about quality?

The guy who polishes the floors.

• • •

We have no trouble spotting sloppy service. I employed a man a few years ago to take care of my yard. I was careful to tell him what I wanted him to do. He did a great job on about 90 percent of the yard. There was always something that he didn't do.

A section of the yard didn't get trimmed by the weed eater.
Some bushes didn't get trimmed.
Some leaves didn't get raked.
Some vines were not cleared away.

He always had an excuse –

The weed eater broke.
Those bushes had poison ivy on them.
All the leaves had been raked when he left. There must have been (very) strong winds that occurred after he left.

Unfortunately, we see this every day, don't we?
Ever had a bad experience in a restaurant?
How about the cleaners?
How about a moving company?
How about a house painter?
How about a hospital?
In every industry, it's easy to experience bad service. That's why good service stands out.

. . .

Saltillo, Tennessee, is a rural, declining community with no industry and no jobs. All types of restaurants had come and gone with no success. Then a Mexican restaurant appeared.

Saltillo did not have a Hispanic population. As a matter of fact, most people in the community could not tell the difference between a burrito and a buffalo. The folks who opened the restaurant did not speak much English. It seemed like an ill-conceived business plan to just about everyone.

When the restaurant opened, business was slim. So, with time on their hands, the employees went out front and washed the cars and trucks of their customers. Word traveled fast. More folks came to try out the new restaurant and hopefully get a car wash.

It didn't hurt that the food was outstanding. Yes, there was a language issue on both sides. The locals had to learn what an enchilada was. They had to see for themselves that this Mexican food, while not meat and potatoes, was very tasty. They noticed the courtesy and patience. They noticed the cleanliness. They noticed the good prices. They noticed the fond welcomes and goodbyes.

The restaurant is still there. So are the customers. It's hard to get a table on Sunday after church. But folks don't mind the wait. It gives them a chance to visit with each other and anticipate what the smells are advertising.

The restaurant exceeds the 90 percent standard. I don't know the help staff, but I *do* know that they have made food preparation and customer service a passion.

God tells us that He wants us to do a good job at whatever we have to do. For me, that means spending the kind of time it takes to:

- teach a good Sunday School lesson
- buy a meaningful birthday present
- clean the house
- write a good book
- be a good son
- be a good father
- be a good husband

Your list might be different. But you get the idea. You and I have to get past what's wrong with life. We have to get past how other folks treat us. And, instead, we must concentrate on doing a good job at whatever it is we have to do.

• • •

I had a conversation last week with a man who said, "I never thought I'd be working this long. Here I am in my 70's, and I can't afford to retire." He's looking at others who have a good retirement and plenty of leisure time. It didn't turn out that way for him.

He's got a decision to make. Does he become bitter and complain and make everyone he comes in contact with pay for his predicament? Or does he do the best job he can at what he must do every day?

I was sharing these thoughts yesterday with a men's prayer group I meet with each Friday morning. When I asked for responses, Bryan Crisman, in his mid-90's, said,

> *My philosophy has always been to look for ways to leave where I am a little better than it was. Maybe that's a big thing like helping someone in a profound way. Maybe it's more simple, like picking up some paper that is on the ground. It's all about how you choose to see life. There are many things I can no longer do in my life, like fly an airplane or even drive a car. But there are things I can do. It's up to me to find those opportunities and do the best I can. By the way, the same is true for each of you young whipper-snappers sitting around this table, too!*

I glorified you on earth, having accomplished the work you gave me to do. John 17:4

Showing Whose Side I'm On

Remember the story of the rich man who tore down his barns to build bigger barns (Luke 12)?

Someone in the crowd said to him, "Teacher, tell my brother to divide the inheritance with me."

Jesus replied, "Man, who appointed me a judge or an arbiter between you?" Then he said to them, "Watch out! Be on your guard against all kinds of greed; life does not consist in an abundance of possessions."

And he told them this parable: "The ground of a certain rich man yielded an abundant harvest. He thought to himself, What shall I do? I have no place to store my crops.

Then he said, This is what I'll do. I will tear down my barns and build bigger ones, and there I will store my surplus grain. And I'll say to myself, You have plenty of grain laid up for many years. Take life easy; eat, drink and be merry.

237

But God said to him, 'You fool! This very night your life will be demanded from you. Then who will get what you have prepared for yourself?'

This is how it will be with whoever stores up things for themselves but is not rich toward God."

Why was God so angry? I think it was because the rich man was focused on himself. The rich man did not ask God what he should do. The rich man was selfish.

I am so tired of greed. I am so tired of selfishness. Ever try to divide an inheritance? It's not pretty. Most people I come into contact with seem more interested in what they can get than the welfare of others.

But there's more to this story.

The question for you and for me is how are we going to use the rest of our lives? Let's say you've worked really hard and have a nest egg and some perks in the form of retirement income, a second home, freedom to travel and freedom from work.

Again, how are you going to spend the rest of your life? You can retire from your career but *can you retire from serving others?*

I have a friend who was able to retire at an early age. How does he handle his retirement? On one day, he volunteers at the church building - painting, cleaning and fixing anything he can. On another day, he volunteers at the theology library, working to help catalog and archive. On another day, he volunteers at the Hospice House. Other days find him helping others in many ways. He has time to exercise and take some trips, but he also makes service a priority.

I have seen him help others with funeral arrangements, with leaves that need to be raked, with houses that need paint, with estate sales, with transportation, with fundraising events and by opening his home for meals and lodging.

As a matter of fact, his plan for many years was to allow his retirement to provide greater service and work for the Lord.

When he reads this, he will be embarrassed and probably ticked that I would single him out. Oh well. He would say that he is not perfect and that he should not be used as an example. While it's true that none of us is perfect, it's also true that this world is not our home. His life reminds me of that. Instead of pointing inwardly, he looks for opportunities to use his resources for others. He points upward.

That type of unselfishness is truly a light in a world of selfish darkness. When you take a look at Matthew 25, Jesus is telling the folks that they are being rewarded for what? Helping others. Regardless of our age, that's what He expects us to do.

At an advanced age, my grandfather gave others rides to church. He continued to teach a Bible class. He and my grandmother continued to invite folks over to eat. He woke up early every morning to read his Bible. He delighted in talking to others about what he read. He gave vegetables from his garden to those who needed it. He made plenty of visits to encourage others.

It ain't over till it's over. We have to hang in there.

As I write this, there's a man who probably won't live to read these words. I hope he does. He is on final approach. And yet, he has continued to help others. He goes to church. He goes to Sunday school. He comes to Wednesday night services. I asked him why. "There are fewer things I can do now to encourage people," he said. "But they can see that I haven't given up. They can see in whom I trust. They can see that I don't think death is the end. I hope my presence encourages them."

Jack Lewis is a prolific writer who goes to our church. He is 96. In the last year, he has written two books, spoken at several conferences and traveled to speak in Japan. Oh yes, and he teaches a Bible class each Sunday. Even though he is feeling the effects of age, he continues to sit at the very front pew at the 8:30 a.m. worship service. When asked why he attends even when he doesn't feel so good and isn't able to read the words in the hymnal or on the screen, he replied,

"I want folks to know whose side I'm on."

But if serving the Lord seems undesirable to you, then choose for yourselves this day whom you will serve, whether the gods your ancestors served beyond the Euphrates, or the gods of the Amorites, in whose land you are living. But as for me and my household, we will serve the Lord. Joshua 24:15

Free From Guilt

Jesus went to the Mount of Olives.

At dawn he appeared again in the temple courts, where all the people gathered around him, and he sat down to teach them. The teachers of the law and the Pharisees brought in a woman caught in adultery. They made her stand before the group and said to Jesus, "Teacher, this woman was caught in the act of adultery. In the Law Moses commanded us to stone such women. Now what do you say?" They were using this question as a trap, in order to have a basis for accusing him.

But Jesus bent down and started to write on the ground with his finger. When they kept on questioning him, he straightened up and said to them, "Let any one of you who is without sin be the first to throw a stone at her." Again he stooped down and wrote on the ground.

At this, those who heard began to go away one at a time, the older ones first, until only Jesus was left, with the woman still standing there. Jesus

243

straightened up and asked her, "Woman, where are they? Has no one condemned you?"

"No one, sir," she said.

"Then neither do I condemn you," Jesus declared. "Go now and leave your life of sin." John 8:1-11

This woman had only the clothes she could grab as they were dragging her out. It is interesting to note that the religious leaders did not follow the entire law. They did not bring the man.

The whole scenario was a trap for Jesus. If Jesus agreed with the Jewish law, He's in violation of the Roman law, which forbids such executions.

But if He agrees with the Roman law, then He's in violation of Jewish law, which requires a penalty of death.

Jesus bent down and began writing something. God touching the earth, similar to God writing the Ten Commandments. I'm told these are the only two times we have recorded of God touching the earth.

Then Jesus said, "Okay, let's do this. The first stone should come from the person without sin. Who is that?"

The stones were to be large enough to inflict pain but not too large to cause instant death.

The Son of God, our Savior, said that He didn't condemn her. What?

Wait a minute. You mean he didn't say:

Well sin has its consequences. ZAP!

Or, *I don't condemn you but I'll always remember this and you'll always be a 2nd rate Christian in my book.*

He said *Go now and leave your life of sin.*

Dave Barry was awakened in his Miami home because his two dogs, Earnest and Zippy, were barking to get to the backyard. When he stumbled out, he found them standing in front of the screened-in porch door. But, as Barry explained, thanks to Hurricane Andrew, most of the screens in the porch were orbiting around the earth. However, the door was still standing. And the dogs were standing in front of it. Instead of simply trotting to the left or right around it, they believed the door was the only way to get in or out.

You know what I think our door is? We don't believe that Jesus has the power to forgive sins. Because if we had that belief, we wouldn't hold sins against each other. Let's be honest - historically conservative Christians have pushed sinners away. We shot our wounded. Just like those folks in the circle, holding the rocks.

But Jesus said that day to that woman, *I don't condemn you. Go and leave your life of sin behind. Sin no more.*

Jesus is greater than our sins. He is our Savior. And a Savior trumps sin. You don't have to carry the burden of a sin you committed 20 years ago. Jesus forgives. And just because you sin, your life is not over. If that were the case, all of our lives would be over.

As we look at the Children of Israel, sometimes they were stuck with the Egyptian mindset. They were no longer slaves, but sometimes they still acted like slaves. You and I can be just as ignorant. There is no door keeping us in. Jesus has set us *free!* And once we realize that, we can accept our forgiveness and start to reach out more to others.

Forgiven = Gratitude

Timothy is a successful business person today. But there was a time when Timothy was sleeping on the couch of a Christian Student Center at the University of Memphis. He had been mugged at the car wash at Southern and Highland. He had little money.

After meeting him, I assessed his skills and determined that he had none. So Reem, a custodian at the Highland Street Church, agreed to show Timothy how to clean a building. He showed him how to mop and sanitize and wax. I sent emails to friends at church, asking if they would let poor Timothy clean their houses. Several said yes.

A doctor and managing partner of a medical group asked Timothy to clean their central office. Then the other locations. Another large medical building in the Wolfchase area asked Timothy if he could clean their building. Timothy had to hire employees. Timothy was no longer poor!

Timothy knows he didn't get started by himself. He knows that others helped him with no ulterior motive. He is a grateful person. It has not been unusual for Timothy to say, "Mr. Steve, what can I do for you?" Even today, I think he would be willing to do whatever he could for me.

What I did is nothing compared to what God has done for me and you. He has given us the gift of eternal life. He has given us forgiveness for our sins. Are we as grateful to Him as Timothy is to me? I would say no. I would say that most of us don't even really believe He has forgiven us. Because if we did, why wouldn't we be more grateful? Why would we not be more obedient? And why would we not be more joyful?

When I read the passage in John about the woman who was dragged to Jesus in her embarrassment and shame, I notice Jesus didn't say, *Well, here's what I'm talking about. Hand me one of those rocks!* Isn't it interesting that God didn't throw a rock? Isn't it interesting that God loved that woman as much as He loved anyone else who was there? Isn't it interesting that Jesus gave her another chance at life? I hope the people in that crowd understood His message.

As Jesus mentioned, the truth sets us free. Part of that truth is that God forgives us. Part of that truth is that we all need forgiveness. Part of that truth is that instead of ganging up on each other, we should be loving each other, building each other up and standing with each other to face adversity because God has set us free from the bondage of sin.

But I really, really hope that one day we will understand His message of forgiveness. When we confess our sins, God does not tolerate piling on. Even if we are caught in sin, God does not tolerate anything but love. Sorry about that, but you and I have to forgive, build up and walk alongside sinners. That is, unless you are without sin.

The action step for this week is to look at your life through the lens that God has provided. You have the freedom to forgive yourself. You have the freedom to make a difference in the lives of others. And the good news is that it can start today. How?

Just live a life of forgiveness, joy, peace, gratitude and obedience. Let others know how grateful you are to God for the debt He paid for you. This is not supposed to be a secret! Treat others the way you would treat Jesus and remember that joy comes from God – not circumstances.

> **There is now no condemnation for those who are in Christ Jesus. For the law of the Spirit of life has set you free in Christ Jesus from the law of sin and death. Romans 8:1-2**

Sweet Bird of Youth

My daughter gave me tickets to go see Crosby, Stills and Nash at the Ryman Auditorium in Nashville, Tennessee. Janet and I were sitting in the balcony, awaiting the show. A young couple sat down next to us. The fellow was explaining to his girlfriend who this group was. He was mentioning some of their songs and a little of their history. I smiled at his enthusiasm for a group that started singing before he was born.

He saw me smiling and asked, "Have you been a fan of theirs for very long?" I nodded and told him that I had grown up with their music and had heard them in concert when I was about his age. He liked that and asked what it was like to live in the 60's and 70's. I shared with him that I worked in the Ryman Auditorium when I was in college and got to hear a lot of historic vocalists.

There was a pause in our conversation, and I couldn't help but imagine how cool he must think I was. It was at that point that his girlfriend turned to me and, in a voice louder than necessary, asked, "COULD YOU TAKE OUR PHOTO?" She produced her phone and asked, "DO YOU KNOW HOW TO USE AN IPHONE?"

My grin froze. I took the picture.

It's amazing how the perception of others can make us feel. As I have thought about it, to determine a person's worth by their age, or lack thereof, is a mistake.

My neighbor would fit in the category of *senior citizen*. Many would say she has little worth. *Her life is almost over,* they would reason. Imagine my surprise when I found out that she is a classical musician, a renowned artist and a very intelligent and humorous person. She has become a good friend since I took off the label. For the time being, I have convinced her to stay off the roof to blow the leaves.

I have also made the assumption that because I am no longer 20, younger folks don't want to have anything to do with me. Now, that is true to a degree. I talked to a young buck not long ago who said that people in their 50's and beyond were not nearly as effective in the pulpit as people under 50. I think he is 37. I wonder how he'll feel in 13 years?

But I can't assume that everyone feels that way. It's similar to what happens when I speak. Some folks think I am hilarious, witty and insightful. Most go away thinking I'm pretty good and it was worth their time. And there are a few who didn't like it.

I have learned in speaking that I can't spend all my energy on trying to win those last folks over. Maybe they don't like the way I look. Maybe they don't like my southern accent. Maybe they don't like my sense of humor. I just have to accept the fact that they can't be changed and be okay with it.

Now, if the truth were known, the fact that a 25-year-old might not want to hang out with me doesn't cause me to lose sleep. But I can't write that person off because of his age any more than he should write me off because of mine.

To paraphrase Jesus, as we treat the oldest or the youngest of these, we treat Him.

Know this, my beloved brothers: let every person be quick to hear, slow to speak and slow to anger. James 1:19

A Friend in Need

Years ago, Joe Priestly was visiting his father in Greenfield, Tennessee. As the old truck pulled into the long, country driveway, Mr. Priestly stopped at the mailbox and told Joe to get out to collect the mail.

Joe opened the mailbox and was immediately swarmed by a community of yellow jackets. Joe rushed back to the truck just in time to see his father lock the door. As Joe was being stung, his father began to pull away from him, explaining that he didn't want the yellow jackets in the truck.

I love that story! I can picture Joe hopping around, fending off the yellow jackets as best he could, and then jumping in the lake. Unfortunately, that's what our "church" friends do sometimes. They are happy to eat with us, sit with us and spend time with us *until* the yellow jackets come. Then they roll up the window and pull away.

As I read passages from the Bible, I understand that actions speak louder than words.

The truth is that our friends are going to make mistakes. The truth is that some of our friends are going to get sick. Or need money. Or have a catastrophe. The question is how will you and I respond? Move on because it's not going to be fun? Stay and help because that's what friends do?

The good news is that we don't have to make that decision. It was decided for us in the words of Jesus (Matthew 25: 31-46).

We need to quit rolling up our windows. We need to quit saying, *Whew! Glad that didn't happen to me!*

If we are going to live like God wants us to, we need to be a friend in good times and bad. A friend in need is a friend.

Two are better than one, because they have a good return for their work. If one falls down, his friend can help him up. But pity the man who falls and has no one to help him up! Ecclesiastes 4:9-10

Things That Help Me

We are told that we are God's temples. We need to take care of ourselves. Here are some activities that help me:

- **I go for a walk in the neighborhood.** I love to see the flowers in the spring, or the leaves change color in the fall. It gives me a chance to think about whatever I need to think about and talk to God. Many studies have shown that sunshine combined with walking raises our mood.

- **I fish.** Most of the time I fish in a boat, but sometimes I sit on the bank and throw a line in the water. It is peaceful and relaxing. The pace slows down, and I am able to think about where things are and where they need to be.

- **I go to the beach.** As I have opportunity, I enjoy going to the beach. It's enjoyable to walk on the sand or walkways close to the beach. The air is fresh, the sun is bright, the sky is blue. I enjoy sitting under an umbrella or seaside porch and listening to the surf. I like to grill steaks and eat them on the porch, in view of the ocean. I enjoy taking a step back and seeing things in perspective.

- **I go to the mountains.** As I write this, I'm looking at the Smoky Mountains in early November. While here, I write, hike, look at the mountains and enjoy God's creation.

- **I go to the country.** I enjoy walking through the trails, watching the deer, the turkey, the hummingbirds and other beautiful birds around. I enjoy sitting around a campfire, cooking over it and then sitting back and looking at the sky with too many stars to count.

- **I go to the zoo.** One of the best investments I've made is in an annual pass to our city's zoo. I try to go at least once a week, not so much to see the animals, but to walk. It's a safe, friendly place. And waving to the animals is also fun. It's not Disney World, but it provides fresh air and pretty neat scenery. Because I go regularly, I'm able to see how the animals act when there are a lot of people and when there are a few. I don't think about too much. I just enjoy the scenery and ask God how He decided on each animal.

- **I spend time with other Christian men.** About once a month, I go with some friends to the movies. These are men I respect. Sometimes we eat ahead of time. At the movies, we have certain rules – we sit with a seat between us, so we can spread out. Romantic movies are not permitted. Many movies are judged by rounds fired per minute. Being around these men is an encouragement to me. We have fun. I also get together with some men every Friday morning for prayer and Bible study. It's helpful.

These are things I do intentionally, to take care of me. Your list may be dramatically different. But if you don't choose, they won't happen. And if they don't happen, you may not be taking care of yourself the way you should. And if you don't take care of yourself, you won't be as much good to others or to the Lord.

A cheerful heart is good medicine, but a crushed spirit dries up the bones. Proverbs 17:22.

Structure in Your Life

Yesterday, Dr. Leon Sanderson and I ate lunch at the invitation of a friend who was having trouble in many areas of his life. He no longer had a job. His savings were drying up. He had health problems. He had gained weight. He had dropped out of his social circle and church family. He had asked to meet with us.

After he told us about his problems, we offered a few suggestions for raising money, getting a job, starting an exercise plan, reconnecting with friends and going back to church. For each of our suggestions, Bob gave a reason for why that wouldn't work.

Leon finally said, "You know, Bob, I have found that in order for me to make any headway in life, I have to have *structure*. I need to know what I'm going to be doing today. I need to know what my goals are for this week, next week and next month. That helps me get up and get going each morning. It helps me know what I need to do to accomplish my goals.

It seems to me that the big thing lacking in your life is *structure*. And worse, you don't seem to want to create structure. Without structure, you're never going to have the kind of life you want."

As I later thought about his words, it occurred to me how profound his thought was. In order to live a life of purpose and achievement, you and I need lives of structure.

Like you, I realize that today is a gift from God. I don't know how many more days He will give me, but I *do* know that I want to use them to make a difference. The kind of difference He wants me to make.

And I have learned that some discipline in life increases my achievement level.

So, what does that mean? How does that work?

I would suggest that you first evaluate what you need to do short term and long term. What are your goals, your dreams, your commitments?

To be a good husband? To be a good father? To draw closer to God? To stay in shape? To be a better neighbor? To help others in a more tangible way?

I applaud those goals. Now, break it down as to what it takes to do that. What are some action steps?

- **Be a good father.** Maybe it's to throw the baseball with your son or volunteer as an assistant coach on his team. Maybe it's to spend every Saturday morning with your daughter, in some mutually planned activities.

- **Be a good husband.** Maybe it's to turn off the TV and take a walk after supper. Maybe it's to read the Bible together for 10 minutes every night. Maybe it's to talk about vacation plans far in advance.

- **Draw closer to God.** Maybe it's to commit to spending a few minutes every morning reading the Bible and talking to God. Maybe it's to join a weekly men's prayer breakfast. Maybe it's having a short family devotional several times a week.

- **Stay in shape.** Maybe it's a membership in the gym (that you actually use) before you get to work, even if that means getting up pretty early. Maybe it means saying no to so many desserts. Maybe it means playing with the kids in the backyard instead of watching so much TV.

- **Be a better neighbor.** Maybe that means learning the neighbors' names on each side of you and across the street. Maybe that means inviting them to come over for a cookout. Maybe it means taking a cake or a pie to a new neighbor. Maybe it means learning birthdays and anniversaries. Maybe it means helping out when a neighbor needs a ride to the doctor or a babysitter.

- **Help others in a more tangible way.** This depends on how you want to help. There is no single way. Maybe you can help others with painting, plumbing, raking, cooking, transportation or just by providing company. Maybe you can invite others to come to your vacation home. Maybe you can provide financial assistance to pay some bills.

You can't do any of that without structure. You have to know what needs to be done. You have to have a plan. And you need to actively use that plan. It requires getting up, getting things done and enjoying the ride.

You're going to do that differently from me. I know of a family that spends the bulk of their resources helping the Village of Hope in Guana. I know of a man who gives most of his income to Harding School of Theology. I know of a man in his 50's who is now retired so that he can spend every day helping others. I know of a family who invites a different family several times a year to their vacation home. Sometimes they go with the family. Sometimes they don't. I know of others who quietly give enough money to pay for a student's tuition to a private Christian school or to a Christian college.

I just know that the more disciplined I am in my life, the more I get done. I cannot wait to be in the mood. I have to get up and get with it. And I have to do that consistently.

This is the day the Lord has made. I want to rejoice and be glad in it. I want to love God and others in the course of today. I want God to be pleased with how I've used the day.

I know that I'm reminding you of something that you already know to do. And I'm excited to hear what you are able to do with what God has entrusted to you.

A man without self-control is like a city broken into and left without walls. Proverbs 25:28

It's Hard to Look Cool
When You Have No Eyebrows

I spent a lot of time in high school with my good friend, Nick Wiser. Nick's house had a sunroom. Its major attraction was the pool table. The room was kept warm in the winter by a gas heater. I remember one time coming over to see Nick.

"I've got to go upstairs for minute," Nick said. "Turn on the heater. The matches are in the kitchen."

"Okay," I said.

I had never lit a gas heater in my life. It was always on when I was there. But I knew it ran on gas. So, how hard could it be?

I turned the gas on and went to the kitchen to find the matches. It took a while, but I found them. On the way back, I stopped to pet the dog. Then I entered the sunroom and stuck the match.

The first thing I saw was light. It surrounded me.
The first thing I heard was a loud noise. It sounded like thunder.
The first thing I smelled was something burning. It was me.

Nick came running in. His look of concern turned into a look of amazement and then a look of extreme amusement.

He was laughing so hard he could barely ask me if I was okay.

I was still recovering from my near-death experience. Nick was not impressed. He simply pointed and said, "Go look in the mirror."

I went to the bathroom. I saw me staring back, with an outer surface of singed hair that looked like a hat, and *no eyebrows*.

Going to school was even worse. It is hard to look cool when you have no eyebrows.

I discovered that when you don't have eyebrows, people tend to stare at you a lot.

Fast forward several decades. I had one of those gizmos to cut your sideburns. I noticed that one of my eyebrows was a little bushy. I guess I wasn't paying as much attention as I should because the next thing I know, half of the eyebrow was gone.

Yes, people noticed. And they weren't very kind with their comments. They thought they were pretty funny.

Maybe that's why I have to remember verses like this:

The Lord does not look at the things man looks at. Man looks at the outward appearance, but the Lord looks at the heart. 1 Samuel 16:7

Some of us age much better than others. And that's just something we have to accept. But I've also learned that outer beauty truly is skin deep.

There are things that are within your control. And there are things that are out of your control. So, what are we to do? Grumble? Get angry? Complain about our bad luck? Take it out on others? Feel like nobody could like us so we just slither around?

Well, that's one way. But another way is to do what we can with what we have. I'll tell you a secret. You and I give others a cue on how to treat us. If we accept ourselves, others will, too. Not only that, they see our inner beauty. Our heart.

It's true.

I praise you, for I am fearfully and wonderfully made. Wonderful are your works; my soul knows it very well. Psalm 139:14

How to Fight a Giant

I was writing a book with Ben Gay. We were driving around in Big Sur, California. Ben turned into a parking space just as another car approached from the opposite direction. The car stopped behind Ben's car, and two guys about the size of Vermont and New Hampshire stepped out of the car.

We got out, too. They told Ben that he needed to move his car. Ben, fearless, informed them that they could forget it. They informed Ben they might have to teach him a lesson. Vermont, for the first time, looked over at me.

"What do you have in your hand?" he, asked.

I looked down. "I think it's a tire tool." I found it under the seat.

New Hampshire looked over at it. "What are you going to do with that?"

"I don't know yet," I said.

"What do you mean by that?" Vermont asked.

"If you stay over there, I won't do anything. But if you come over here,

I'll probably hit you on the side of your head with it."

"I don't think you would," New Hampshire said.

I shook my head. "I'm sorry," I said. "I'm from Tennessee, so I don't know about any rules you might have in California. But in Tennessee, you can use a tire tool."

Well, I knew they had talked way too much if they were going to mix it up. As a matter of fact, they ended up sitting two tables away from us at the restaurant, and Ben even bought their dinner.

In I Samuel 17, we read about David facing a much larger man. It's a familiar story. While everyone else was afraid, David was angry. He wanted to take care of Goliath and knew that God would help him do just that. The question that was on King Saul's mind was *how?* On paper, David had no chance. He was outmatched in every category.

We all have our giants. I don't know what yours are, but I know there are many to battle.

Loneliness.
Grief.
Money.
Guilt.
Fear.

Giants come in all shapes.

Maybe you've lost your way.
Maybe you don't like who you've become.

Maybe you feel taken for granted.
Maybe you don't think you're making a difference.
Maybe you've been hurt deeply.
Maybe you see no way out.
Maybe you just feel outmatched.

I was with a friend yesterday whose life has crumbled. He's facing a giant. On paper, he's not going to come out of this. He's outmatched in every category.

I have a friend at church who has cancer. He's getting weaker every week. He's facing a giant. On paper, he's not going to come out of this. He's outmatched, and the game is about to be over.

Goliath didn't see David's secret weapon. He commented on the staff, but not on the rocks.

But David's secret weapon was not rocks and a sling. It was God. He believed that God was with him. He believed that God heard him. He knew that God was aware of his circumstances. He trusted that God would help him overcome the giant that stood in front of him.

You have to believe that the same God who loved David loves you just as much. You have to believe that He is with you and that He hears you just as clearly as He heard David. He knows what's standing in front of you. And He is just as able to slay your giants. You have to trust Him as much as David did.

On paper it may look pretty one-sided. But God tells us to trust Him. He is greater than our giants. We cannot think of it from the human side, but from God's vantage point. He is able and willing to help us.

But he requires our absolute trust.

Trust in the Lord with all your heart; do not depend on your own understanding. Seek His will in all you do, and He will show you which path to.
Proverbs 3:5-6

The Value of a Guide

Hank and I went down the Ocoee River near Chattanooga. They used it for the Olympics a few years ago because the rapids were Categories 4 and 5. We chose the High Country Adventures Outfitters. They gave us helmets. They showed us how to paddle. The guide showed us how to get down in the bottom of the raft when we hit major turbulence. He showed us how to hold on.

"When I say paddle, you have to paddle as hard as you can, even if it doesn't seem to make sense. When I say *get down,* you must do it immediately."

We did what he said, and we did not capsize or fall out of the boat. Even though the current was really fierce at times, we made it fine. Our guide knew how to attack the currents. He knew where the submerged rocks were. And he knew how to keep from turning over.

As we were riding back in the bus to the outfitter station, I asked our guide if he ever had boats capsize. He smiled and said, "If they don't do what I tell them to, they will flip or fall out."

He paused for a second and said, "And if I don't like their attitude, I can flip them or hit a rock just hard enough to make a certain passenger go flying out of the boat. *Folks don't give the guide enough credit.*"

As I thought about that later, I reflected on the 23rd Psalm.

The Lord is my shepherd, I lack nothing.
He makes me lie down in green pastures,
He leads me beside quiet waters,
He refreshes my soul.
He guides me along the right paths

**for his name's sake.
Even though I walk
through the darkest valley,
I will fear no evil,
for you are with me;
your rod and your staff,
they comfort me.**

Are you in a Category 5 rapid? Do you ever say, *God where are you?
You tell me to pray, but I don't see any results.*

Life doesn't always make sense. The loss of a loved one. A loved one
rejecting you. Sickness. Pain. Loneliness. Heartache.

And God's commandments are sometimes puzzling. Love those who
hate you. Return good for evil. Pray without ceasing.

And so we go on. A day at a time. An hour. A minute. We have to
keep living. Even if it feels like all the lights in the whole world just
went off, we have to get up, get dressed and continue our lives. We
have to believe that God is close to the brokenhearted and those who
are crushed in spirit (Psalm 34:18).

We have to help others who go through this pain. We have to believe
that there is more to life than what we see.

You and I need a guide just as much as Hank and I needed a guide
going down the rapids of the Ocoee. His directions may not always
make sense. We don't understand every command. We just have to
trust that He knows more about the way home than we do.

But the eyes of the Lord are on those who fear him, on those whose hope is in his unfailing love.
Psalm 33:18

Rain

As I write, it is raining. I am taken back to a time when I was in Boy Scouts. We were camping on land owned by Dr. Herman LaVelle in Fayette County, Tennessee. We were proud of our tents, recently donated by a parent. They were teepees. They were about 12 feet tall and maybe 8 feet wide. They looked great!

We had a lot of fun that night, thinking about what it must have been like to live in a teepee. Because there was a hole in the top, we thought it would have been great to have a campfire in our teepee. Our Scoutmaster, Mr. Van, didn't agree, so we didn't have one.

Then the rain came. It was a gully washer, complete with thunder and lightning. The hole in the top of the tent wasn't such a great feature at that point. The four of us sleeping in our tent, huddled to one side, sitting on a couple of sleeping bags, and holding the others on top of our heads. By the end of the endless night, everything was soaked, including us.

I've camped in the rain several times after that. It's never fun to pack up a wet tent. I remember when Hank and I were camping in north Mississippi. It rained. The tent was soaked. Rather than pack it up, we decided to let it dry and come back the next day.

Well, when we did, we discovered that the tent had been destroyed. Someone had run over it multiple times with his vehicle. You could see the tire tracks on the tent. I followed the tracks. They headed down to the lake. But there were no return tracks. When we got down to the lake, we found a Jeep with no one in it. It was stuck in the mud.

We had several options. I took the high road and called the Sheriff. The dispatcher sent the wrong message out, it seems, because in a very short period of time, we heard sirens heading our way from every direction. Instead of reporting that there was a Jeep stuck in the mud, the dispatcher said there was a Jeep stuck in the lake and emergency assistance was needed to help the passengers.

The first responders were Southaven Police cars. Then there were the fire trucks. Then the ambulances. Even the Desoto County Dive Team! I think every vehicle with a flashing light and siren in the county came to the lake. They seemed disappointed when they saw the Jeep in the mud beside the lake. When they saw the tire tracks on the destroyed tent, they shared my anger and disgust.

Within an hour, the perpetrator was identified and taken into custody.

I have been in a backpacker's tent with my friend, Dr. Tom Fox, at about 13,000 feet in the Wind River Region of Wyoming, when a terrible storm fell on top of us. Lightning was striking within 100 feet of our tent. When you are on top of a very high mountain, in a tent, in the middle of a thunderstorm, you're the target for those lightning bolts!

The lightning was so close that we heard the sound at the same time it hit. We could smell it! We just prayed that God would spare us, and He did.

I've been in a tornado when I was in college in Nashville. I was taking my girlfriend, Liz Dorris, back to the dorm. We were coming back from church on Wednesday night. The tornado flipped other cars over in the parking lot. It skipped over us. We watched as the windows on my car sucked inward. We could feel the car move. We heard the deafening roar. We survived without a scratch.

I've heard cliches about the rain – *Into each life, a little rain must fall.* Or – *the rain falls on the just and the unjust.* As I look at this rain today, I am reminded that some parts of life are sunny with blue skies. Some are cloudy and depressing. Sometimes it's a light shower, and sometimes a heavy storm.

As you read this today, you are experiencing one of the above, not just out the window, but in your life. God tells us that He will not forsake us, despite the conditions. He is there in good times and bad. And He expects us to remember Him not just in the bad times, but also in the good.

Be strong and courageous. Do not fear or terrified because of them, for the Lord your God who goes with you. He will not leave you nor forsake you. Deuteronomy 31:6

Smiling All the Way to Heaven

The date was Bison Day, October, 1974. The place was Burton Alumni Auditorium, David Lipscomb College, Nashville, Tennessee.

Since David Lipscomb didn't have a football team, they made a big deal out of the first game of basketball season. All of the social clubs wore costumes, and school spirit was whipped into a frenzy.

Our college fraternity chose a Cowboy theme. We dressed up like cowboys. Those of us who could grew mustaches. We created a performance which would later become known as the first ever Tau Phi Cowboy Show, directed by yours truly. It has been held annually ever since. If you're looking for my plaque on the wall, let me save you some time. It ain't there.

In an effort to garner interest for our show, and because it seemed fun to do, we arranged for one of our members, Ed, a.k.a. Snort, to do something rather unusual.

Being a Christian college, Lipscomb held chapel every day in the auditorum. Chapel usually opened with greetings from Dr. Willard Collins, the vice president of the school (later president) and a very popular administrator with the student body.

As the details of what happened unfold, let me remind you that things have changed in this world since 1974. You'll see what I mean.

I asked Dr. Collins if we could have some fun with our homecoming chapel. He said yes.

It was to go like this:

As Dr. Collins read announcements, which I had fictionalized for him, Snort was to walk down the aisle, in his cowboy attire, complete with a cowboy hat, cowboy shirt, chaps, boots, spurs and a six-shooter in the holster.

He was to interrupt Brother Collins, saying, "Willard Collins, I'm calling you out."

We knew the student body would be stunned or perhaps interrupted from study. Either way, they would be entertained.

At this point, Dr. Collins was to say, "Son, you need to sit down. Can't you see that chapel is in session?"

Snort was to continue, encouraging Willard to draw.

After a couple of more efforts, Willard was to pull his six-shooter (that shot caps) out from behind the podium and shoot Snort. Snort would fall with drama, and Willard would put on his cowboy hat, yell *Go Bisons!* and acknowledge the thunderous applause.

What we didn't know was that during the night, a student's grandmother had passed away. What Willard Collins did not tell Snort was that his announcement was for real. So Snort began walking down the aisle as Willard was offering condolences to this student and her family. Snort had his hand out to his side, walking bowlegged down the aisle of the auditorium, just about to call Dr. Collins out. That's when a fellow member of our club figured out what was going on, made a dive for Snort and stuck him in a seat.

Except for a few startled students who saw the escapade, the tragedy was averted. No lives were lost, besides the grandmother's, that day.

As I have thought about that episode through the years, I always smile. I believe God smiles, too. There are just funny things that happen in life. I think a Creator who created the zebra and the porcupine and the baboon has a sense of humor.

This is the day the Lord has made. Let us rejoice and be glad in it. There is enough sadness to go around already. You and I have to be connoisseurs of joy. We need to laugh and look for things to smile about.

Maybe it's that kitten you can't watch enough.
Maybe it's your basset hound who has the world's greatest howl.
Maybe it's that man who goes to sleep every Sunday at church.
Maybe it's the latest fashion.
Maybe it's laughing at yourself. Plenty of material there. The time that spider scared you and you screamed like an 8-year-old girl.

• • •

I was in Mrs. Annabelle Chumney's home one Sunday after church. We were there to serve her communion. After reading a Bible verse,

289

I led a prayer for the bread and Mrs. Chumney burst out laughing. I asked her what was so funny.

"Your hair," she said. "I'm not used to seeing it gray."

• • •

The police charged into Jimmy Moffett's church building, in search of a criminal, one night during a staff meeting. Brother Moffett volunteered to guide them, but the big Sergeant said no.

"Well, there are some things you need to be careful about in this church building," Jimmy said.

The Sergeant gave him his best cop stare and said, "Thank you. We can probably handle it."

Several minutes went by, and Jimmy heard the *squish-squish-squish* long before the Sergeant appeared.

"You didn't tell me about the baptistry."

Jimmy just smiled.

• • •

One day I was called to come over to my parents' house. My father, already in hospice, thought his time had come. So, the family sat around his bed for a couple of hours.

He motioned for me to come over. "I think I've made a mistake.

Looks like I may have been a little premature in asking the family to gather around."

I nodded.

"How are we going to get out of this?" he asked.

I assured him everyone would understand.

He cleared his throat and said, "Could I have everyone's attention please. It looks like I'm not going to die right now. You can go back home. Thank you for coming."

• • •

As Christians, we know the end of the story, and it's a good one. We can have the peace that passes understanding. We can take deep breaths, despite our circumstances. And we can laugh in the middle of sadness.

I love to hear a good story. Good stories usually make me laugh. I want to smile and laugh and share that joy with others while I can. Whether I'm in a boat, on the porch, by the campfire or the fireplace, by a sick bed, walking through the woods, at the ballgame or standing in the stream with a pole in my hands, I enjoy God's creation. I like to share good times and laughter with others.

Maybe we can't take everything with us when we die, but I think the memories of joy and laughter might be an exception. Joy should not be conditional. We can be glad in the day the Lord has made regardless of our circumstances.

I want to smile all the way to Heaven.

You make known to me the path of life; in your presence there is fullness of joy; at your right hand are pleasures forevermore. Psalm 16:11

A Step Back to Look Forward

One of my favorite activities in the fall is to admire trees. I love Maples. As a matter of fact, there is a beautiful Maple tree that I can see from the window here in my office. It was a brilliant yellow. It has now turned to shades of orange. And even though today's temperature is below freezing and there's a dusting of snow on the ground, the tree is still a beautiful bouquet of colors.

Another tree that I love during the fall is the Ginko. There's a magnificent Ginko that I go past most days on my walk. Its leaves turn from green to a brilliant yellow. When they fall off the tree, they seem to do it all at once, leaving a beautiful yellow carpet for a few of days.

We were in the Smokies this year in the peak of fall foliage. Then came an unexpected snowstorm. The beauty of the fall leaves with snow on the ground was absolutely breath taking.

I'm thinking of a day during that trip when Janet and I took a walk through the trees. On one side was a very cold gurgling stream, filled with large boulders that had been rounded by time. You could hear the wind above us. We couldn't feel it, due to the trees and mountains around, but we could see leaves that were falling because of it.

We sat down on the big rocks to enjoy the moment. The birds flew

to the creek to get a drink of water and search for a minnow or a bug. We could hear them sing to each other. Sunlight was peaking through the trees. I didn't see any trout, but I knew some were close by. We saw a couple of wood ducks that were swimming upstream. I did not want to leave. But I could also feel the cold rocks through my jeans, so I guess it was time.

As a lover of nature, I am reminded of God when I am in that kind of setting. I hope Heaven resembles the Smokies. I can't imagine the place we'll spend eternity without trees and water. I hope we can build campfires and camp out. I'm glad we can now.

It is good for me to take a step back and think about God, especially when I get to do that in the midst of a beautiful scene. There are a couple of large parks in Memphis that I enjoy visiting. I can take long walks there without seeing a soul and think about His will for my life. I also enjoy sitting on our deck soaking in the sounds of nature. If you want to get me a Christmas present, I could use a fire pit.

I like quiet. I like relaxing. I like getting away. I like spending time with family. I like reading a book on the beach or the balcony or in the woods. I like telling stories around the campfire. I like fishing in a boat or by the side of a pond. I like hiking. I like eating a trail meal on the side of a mountain.

I believe you need to know how you enjoy retreats and vacations. And feel okay if you like something that someone else doesn't. Perhaps most importantly, you need to plan these retreats and vacations a few times each year.

I agree that we need to work hard. I agree that there is nothing virtuous about being lazy. There is too much to do before our lives are over. But I also believe that we need to stop occasionally. We need to take time to enjoy God's creation. We need to think about where we are, where we've been, and where we're going. We need to take a step back and ask God for guidance.

So, I plan three or four getaways each year. It may not surprise you that most of these involve cabins. Some by rivers and lakes. Some on top of mountains.

As I've mentioned, for many years I've rented a cabin in the mountains during Christmas season for a week. We've made a lot of memories on those trips. One year, the snow was so bad we barely made it up to the cabin. We were snowbound for several days. We made a sled and cooked over the fireplace. Twice, my parents went with us. They loved it as much as we did. We still have the photos to remind us of those times.

Over the years, Hank and I have camped a lot. As he got older (or maybe as I got older), we seem to be staying in cabins or state park inns more. But we camped in all kinds of weather. We camped in all types of locations. And we had a blast.

Getting away doesn't have to be expensive. As a matter of fact, it doesn't have to cost anything. But you pay a lot for not getting away. After a lifetime of memories, I can tell you that it's worth your investment.

And he said to them, "Come away by yourselves to a desolate place and rest a while." For many were coming and going, and they had no leisure even to eat. Mark 6:31

You're the Greatest!

I wrote a book with Frank Maguire: *You're the Greatest!* In it, Frank tells the story of hiring Ted Koppel as a young reporter at ABC. It was a chance on Frank's part, but Ted did well.

Sometimes when Frank would walk out of his office, Ted would be waiting for him, at his desk. He would talk to Frank about upcoming broadcasts. Then Frank would leave him with his signature farewell – a thumbs up and *You're the greatest!*

Twenty-five years later, ABC had a reunion at Charles Osgood's home. Ted asked Frank to sit down and told him that if he had ever amounted to anything in broadcasting, it was due to Frank giving him a chance early in his career. He said that Frank had faith in him when no one else did.

Frank thanked him and continued to enjoy the afternoon. Frank had to leave a little early and was going to slip out quietly. As he opened the door to leave, someone said, "Hey everybody, Frank's leaving!"

Frank said his goodbyes and then he heard Ted's voice from across the room.

"Hey, Frank . . . tell me one more time."

The room was quiet. Frank looked at Ted for a second, and with tears in his eyes, stuck up his thumb and said,

"Ted, you're the greatest!"

As I spent time with Frank at his home in West Lake Village, California, I noticed that he used this phrase a lot. To the man at the dry cleaners who handed Frank his freshly cleaned suits:

Harvey, you're the greatest!

To the teenager at Baskin Robbins who served Frank:

Francine, you're the greatest!

I've seen him say it to musicians, entertainers, business leaders, waitresses, flight attendants and celebrities. They brightened up when he said it.

With Frank, it was a habit and a lifestyle. The reason it was so effective was that he meant it.

I liked for him to say it to me, too. I liked to hear him say it to others. There's a lesson in there for me. To communicate to others that I like them. To let them know that they are okay. To articulate that I appreciate them.

That should be our message because that is God's message to you and me. *You're the greatest!* He demonstrated that love by creating us and then by paying our debt with Jesus. He demonstrates it now by being with us and continues to demonstrate it by allowing us to live with

Him for eternity. Because He says it to us, we can say it to others.

Toward Frank's final years, he was asked to speak to large audiences throughout the world. What a great storyteller he was. He used those opportunities to teach life lessons. He was passionate. He was humble. And he loved to be with others and help them discover the light behind their eyes.

He always ended his talks with his hand stretched toward the audience with a thumb straight up. Then he would utter the words I commend to you:

You're the greatest!

The one who blesses others is blessed; those who help others are helped. Proverbs 11:25

About Those Shepherds in the Field

As I write this, it is December 18th. Christmas is in one week.

I grew up in an era when everyone seemed to have an aluminum Christmas tree. I remember ours. It was silver with blue balls. There was also a spotlight with a revolving plastic grill of four colors. It really was festive.

Often, we read the second chapter of Luke during the Christmas season. Even Charlie Brown reads it in his Christmas special. It describes shepherds. These were men whose skin had been hardened by the weather. They stood between the sheep and large wild animals. They had very basic weapons. These were fearless men.

And they were about to experience the strangest night of their lives. They were in the field, as usual. Keeping an ear out for any distressed sound coming from their charges. They were sitting around the campfire, telling stories, looking at the immense horizon. This had been their routine for years. The great outdoors was their home.

The angel appeared. And there was light. For the first time in years, they were terrified. The angel told them not to be afraid. Then he told them about a Savior who had been born. In a manger. In Bethlehem. Suddenly the whole sky was filled with angels. Then they left.

It was quiet. Stars once again filled the sky. These men were quiet. Maybe the sheep were quiet, too. When the shepherds had collected their thoughts, they agreed. They needed to go to Bethlehem.

Which brings me to the latest funeral I've been to. It was yesterday. A man lying in a casket. His children and grandchildren were grieving. His wife said to me, "He was my best friend."

Or the conversation I had with a man a few days ago who had made a terrible mistake and asked if I thought God could forgive him.

Or the woman I talked to earlier this week whose husband told her he wanted a divorce after 30 years of marriage.

That's why that angel was in the middle of nowhere, talking to those shepherds. It wasn't about a cute baby. It was about *hope*!

As you read this, you may be going through a difficult time. In the wilderness. Maybe life has not turned out the way you planned. Maybe you've been hurt deeply. Maybe you've hurt someone else deeply. Maybe you are so lonely, you ache. Maybe you feel like a nobody that nobody wants to be with. Maybe you have no idea how you're going to pay this month's bills. Maybe you are in an unhappy family and you don't know how to fix it. Maybe you're very sick.

Whatever your situation, wherever you are, Jesus was born that night to give you *hope*. Three decades later, He would be killed on a cross to give you *hope*. It was a very different ending from the beginning.

You may feel that you don't count because nobody else thinks you're worth anything. You may have distanced yourself from others. Others may not even know you're alive. Sounds a lot like those shepherds. Isn't it interesting that the angels approached men in a remote spot who were forgotten?

God knows about your situation. He is the only one who truly knows how you feel. He knows you better than you know yourself. And He loves you so much that He wants you to live with Him forever. Need proof? Consider that the Creator of everything allowed His son to be murdered by His creation.

Because of that act of love, everything will be okay for you.

My friend, Josh Patrick, who is struggling with cancer, sent a message this morning:

> This present moment – as in right now – is a great gift. Don't squander it by regretting the past or worrying about the future. Jesus removed your condemnation and secured your future. He is closer to you than the blood in your veins. Let him redeem your story. Trust Him.

Have you been hurt? It's going to be okay.
Have you made mistakes? It's going to be okay.
Are you lonely? Afraid? Worried? It's going to be okay.
Are you counting down the last few days of life? It's going to be okay.

Those angels were not just celebrating Jesus' birth. They were celebrating the *hope* He gave you and me.

Jesus was born in humble surroundings. He died in cruel

circumstances. And He arose in victory over everything horrific in this world.

I hope you believe that. If you do, you understand a little more of what the angels meant when they said:

Glory to God in the Highest!
A Savior is born!
A Savior reigns!

And now, we can shout that, too!
In whatever circumstance you are in.
It's going to be okay!

That means we can rejoice in the day the Lord has made.

Therefore do not be anxious, saying, "What shall we eat?" or "What shall we drink?" or "What shall we wear?" For the Gentiles seek after all these things, and your heavenly Father knows that you need them all. But seek first the kingdom of God and his righteousness, and all these things will be added to you. Therefore do not be anxious about tomorrow, for tomorrow will be anxious for itself. Sufficient for the day is its own trouble. Matthew 6:31-34

Acknowledgements

I want to thank my daughter, Brittney Williford, for once again providing the interior and exterior book design, as well as general editing and counsel. We began this journey when Brittney was a very young child with me reading children's books to her. And now, we're working on books together. The book is much better with her management. Thank you Brittney!

I asked my friend Greg Muse to look over a draft of this book. He returned a line and content edit that made the stories much clearer. I had no idea of his talent. Greg, I am grateful for your time and help. I am thankful for your friendship as we share the trail.

I would also recognize the men who have stood beside me in all seasons of my life. I have been honored to share your joys and troubles, and humbled that you shared mine. This includes my Friday morning prayer group, as well as other friends who are closer than brothers.

About the Author

Stephen Williford has written many books, including:

365 Devotionals for Children
When You REALLY Embarrass Yourself Nobody EVER Forgets
Show and Tell; Lessons from A Speech Coach

He enjoys listening to the stories of others under a porch, on the trail, in a boat, or by a campfire. He lives in Memphis, Tennessee. To learn more about him, how to order books or how to secure him as a speaker, visit stephenwilliford.com.

CPSIA information can be obtained
at www.ICGtesting.com
Printed in the USA
LVOW01s1325290116

472140LV00001B/1/P